Math
Made Easy
Second Grade

Progress Chart

This chart lists all the topics in the book. Once you have completed each page, mark the correct box below.

Page	Topic		Page	Topic		Page	Topic	
4	Counting by 1s, 10s, and 100s		14	Subtracting		24	Picture graphs	
5	Counting by 2s		15	Estimating length		25	Equations	
6	Odd and even		16	Addition properties		26	Location on grid	
7	Reading and writing numbers		17	Add or subtract?		27	Placing on grid	
8	Fact families		18	Subtracting		28	Counting by 3s, 4s, and 5s	
9	Fractions		19	Working with coins		29	Adding	
10	Money		20	Money problems		30	Comparing and ordering	
11	Adding		21	Measurement problems		31	Comparing and ordering	
12	Adding		22	Naming 2-dimensional shapes		32	Missing addends	
13	Subtracting		23	Sorting 2-dimensional shapes		33	Reading tables	

Page	Topic		Page	Topic		Page	Topic	
34	Extending geometric patterns		44	2-dimensional shapes		54	Adding	
35	Adding		45	Properties of polygons		55	Subtracting	
36	Adding		46	Pictographs		56	Money problems	
37	Subtracting		47	Most likely/ least likely		57	Measurement problems	
38	Multiplication as repeated addition		48	Square corners		58	Parts of a set	
39	Choose the operation		49	Square corners		59	Bar graphs and pictographs	
40	Venn diagrams		50	Place value		60	Symmetry	
41	Working with coins		51	Fractions of shapes		61	Symmetry	
42	Money problems		52	Finding patterns		62	Doubles	
43	Measurement problems		53	Adding		63	Addition grid	

Well done! With the help of the Captain America, Spider-Man, Black Widow, and other Marvel heroes and villains, you can now count yourself a math expert!

Counting by 1s, 10s, and 100s

Finish each row.

Count by 1s.	24	25	26	27	28	29
Count by 10s.	31	41	51	61	71	81
Count by 100s.	134	234	334	434	534	634

Finish each row. Count by 1s.

21	22	23					
49	50	51					
81	82	83					
35	36	37					
67	68					73	

Finish each row. Count by 10s.

7	17	27					
28	38	48					
73	83	93					
12	22	32					
135	145		165				
321			351				

Finish each row. Count by 100s.

173	273	373					
495	595	695					
733	833	933					
248	348	448					
663	763	863				1,363	

Counting by 2s

| Count by 2s. | 12 | 14 | 16 | 18 | 20 | 22 |
| Count by 2s. | 31 | 33 | 35 | 37 | 39 | 41 |

Finish each row. Count by 2s.

14	16	18				
33	35	37				
17	19	21				
56	58	60				
12	14				24	
79		83				93

Finish each row. Count by 2s.

70						84
31						45
22						36
58						72
45						59
69						83

Finish each row. Count by 2s.

				28			34
			52			58	
					93		97
	8		12				
					19	21	
		60		66			

Odd and even

Circle the numbers that are even.

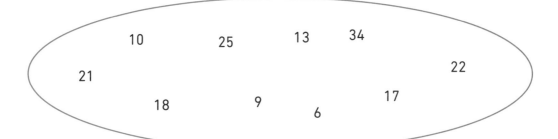

10   25   13   34

21   22

18   9   17

6

Circle the numbers that are odd.

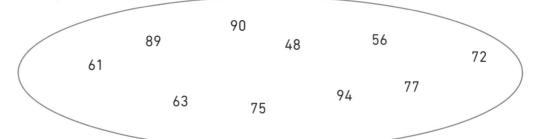

90

89   48   56

61   72

63   75   94   77

Write the odd numbers between 20 and 40.

Write the even numbers between 51 and 71.

Reading and writing numbers

Write this number in words.   278 *two hundred seventy-eight*

Write this number in digits.   four hundred twelve   412

Write each of these numbers in words.

334

689

125

917

Write each of these numbers in digits.

two hundred ninety-nine

six hundred seventy-three

four hundred twelve

eight hundred eighty-six

Write each of these numbers in words.

220

607

817

Write each of these numbers in digits.

three hundred eighteen

eight hundred two

six hundred nineteen

Fact families

Finish the fact family for this group of numbers.

9

5   4

5 + 4 =	9
4 + 5 =	9
9 – 4 =	5
9 – 5 =	4

Finish the fact family for each group of numbers.

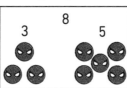   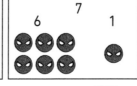   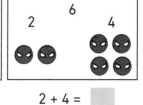

7
4   3

8
3   5

7
6   1

6
2   4

4 + 3 =   3 + 5 =   6 + 1 =   2 + 4 =

3 + 4 =   5 + 3 =   1 + 6 =   4 + 2 =

7 – 3 =   8 – 5 =   7 – 1 =   6 – 4 =

7 – 4 =   8 – 3 =   7 – 6 =   6 – 2 =

5
2   3

9
7   2

3
1   4

8
6   2

2 + 3 =   7 + 2 =   3 + 1 =   6 + 2 =

3 + 2 =   2 + 7 =   1 + 3 =   2 + 6 =

5 – 2 =   9 – 2 =   4 – 1 =   8 – 2 =

5 – 3 =   9 – 7 =   4 – 3 =   8 – 6 =

10   5

6   3

4   2

4   8

5 + 5 =   3 + 3 =   2 + 2 =   4 + 4 =

10 – 5 =   6 – 3 =   4 – 2 =   8 – 4 =

Finish the fact family for each group of numbers.

3
10   7

9
3   6

8
6   2

7
5   2

Fractions

Color one-third (⅓) of each shape.

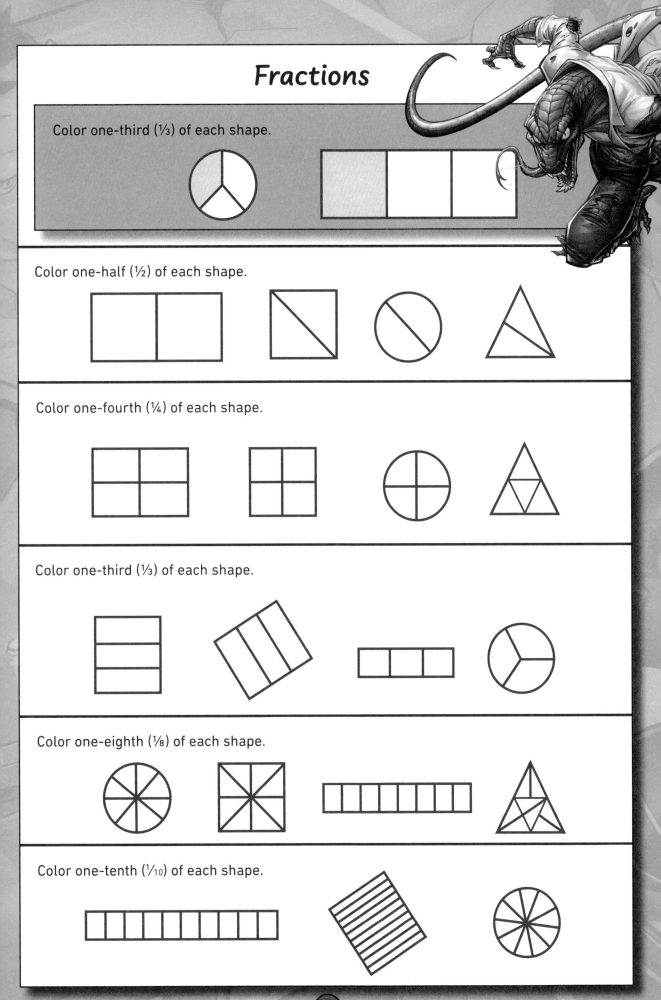

Color one-half (½) of each shape.

Color one-fourth (¼) of each shape.

Color one-third (⅓) of each shape.

Color one-eighth (⅛) of each shape.

Color one-tenth ($\frac{1}{10}$) of each shape.

Money

Change the amount into dollars.   298¢ $2.98

Change each amount into dollars and cents.

276¢ [ ]   415¢ [ ]   190¢ [ ]

124¢ [ ]   776¢ [ ]   283¢ [ ]

987¢ [ ]   300¢ [ ]   908¢ [ ]

515¢ [ ]   819¢ [ ]   678¢ [ ]

Change each amount into cents.

$2.38 [ ] $4.59 [ ] $1.09 [ ]

$5.45 [ ] $9.99 [ ] $6.75 [ ]

$700 [ ] $2.38 [ ] $8.09 [ ]

$3.87 [ ] $8.26 [ ] $7.77 [ ]

Change each amount into dollars and cents.

235¢ [ ]   872¢ [ ]   559¢ [ ]

121¢ [ ]   680¢ [ ]   761¢ [ ]

987¢ [ ]   349¢ [ ]   876¢ [ ]

450¢ [ ]   801¢ [ ]   200¢ [ ]

Change each amount into cents.

$2.90 [ ] $3.97 [ ] $9.05 [ ]

$9.01 [ ] $8.76 [ ] $10.00 [ ]

$3.20 [ ] $5.00 [ ] $5.90 [ ]

$9.11 [ ] $0.80 [ ] $6.66 [ ]

Adding

Write the answer in the box.   35 + 20 =   55

Write the answer in the box.

22 + 16 =   12 + 28 =   80 + 19 =

49 + 23 =   22 + 59 =   23 + 42 =

30 + 40 =   69 + 13 =   18 + 62 =

36 + 61 =   52 + 68 =   12 + 39 =

Write the answer in the box.

20 + 30 + 18 =   40 + 20 + 17 =

65 + 10 + 12 =   77 + 10 + 7 =

35 + 45 + 12 =   70 + 20 + 12 =

40 + 30 + 20 =   49 + 18 + 17 =

43 + 23 + 13 =   28 + 27 + 26 =

81 + 10 + 3 =   50 + 28 + 12 =

Write the answer in the box.

83¢ + 10¢ =   63¢ + 34¢ =   55¢ + 30¢ =

70¢ + 17¢ =   70¢ + 19¢ =   60¢ + 19¢ =

25¢ + 5¢ =   18¢ + 17¢ =   39¢ + 25¢ =

49¢ + 18¢ =   68¢ + 18¢ =   54¢ + 12¢ =

Write the answer in the box.

18 ft + 18 ft + 60 ft =   19 ft + 20 ft + 35 ft =

15 ft + 17 ft + 19 ft =   35 ft + 30 ft + 25 ft =

Adding

Write the answers between the lines.

27	12	69
+ 8	+ 6	+ 9
35	18	78

Write the answers between the lines.

15	23	11	36
+ 9	+ 3	+ 7	+ 5

33	62	44	28
+ 9	+ 5	+ 4	+ 8

36	27	38	27
+ 1	+ 9	+ 2	+ 2

Write the answers between the lines.

12	28	23	18
+ 12	+ 27	+ 33	+ 33

43	38	24	45
+ 43	+ 27	+ 66	+ 23

63	15	73	14
+ 13	+ 29	+ 10	+ 19

Subtracting

Write the answers in the boxes.

13 - 7 = 6   23 - 21 = 2

Write the answers in the boxes.

25 – 4 =	34 – 6 =	24 – 5 =	15 – 8 =
12 – 1 =	21 – 15 =	36 – 12 =	34 – 6 =
44 – 14 =	24 – 17 =	55 – 12 =	18 – 0 =
13 – 6 =	45 – 7 =	23 – 13 =	12 – 7 =
27 – 11 =	13 – 11 =	18 – 12 =	33 – 12 =

Write the answers in the boxes.

22¢ – 2¢ =	18¢ – 7¢ =	99¢ – 34¢ =	23¢ – 16¢ =
65¢ – 36¢ =	22¢ – 11¢ =	30¢ – 23¢ =	88¢ – 17¢ =
89¢ – 35¢ =	56¢ – 46¢ =	47¢ – 29¢ =	46¢ – 13¢ =
65¢ – 23¢ =	63¢ – 9¢ =	84¢ – 34¢ =	55¢ – 42¢ =
47¢ – 9¢ =	19¢ – 11¢ =	63¢ – 26¢ =	72¢ – 12¢ =

Write the answers in the boxes.

How much less than
34¢ is 11¢?

How much less than
40 in. is 26 in.?

Take 16¢ away from 30¢.

War Machine has 50¢. He
spends 40¢ on candy. How
much does he have left?

How much is 60¢ minus 14¢?

Take away 28¢ from 44¢.

What is the difference
between 90 in. and 55 in.?

What is the difference
between 70¢ and 25¢?

Subtracting

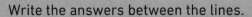

Write the answers between the lines.

26	41	50
− 16	− 24	− 27
10	17	23

Write the answers between the lines.

37	51	70	63
− 24	− 35	− 47	− 48

42	55	43	60
− 24	− 36	− 30	− 37

57	35	73	46
− 38	− 16	− 54	− 38

38	53	60	58
− 26	− 45	− 36	− 47

63	47	80	55
− 45	− 38	− 57	− 48

50	70	51	64
− 18	− 36	− 24	− 46

Estimating length

Circle the longest string.

Circle the shortest string.

Circle the longest string.

Look at the ruler. Circle the closest measure.

1 inch

2 inches   3 inches   4 inches

2 inches   3 inches   4 inches   6 inches

2 inches   3 inches   4 inches   6 inches

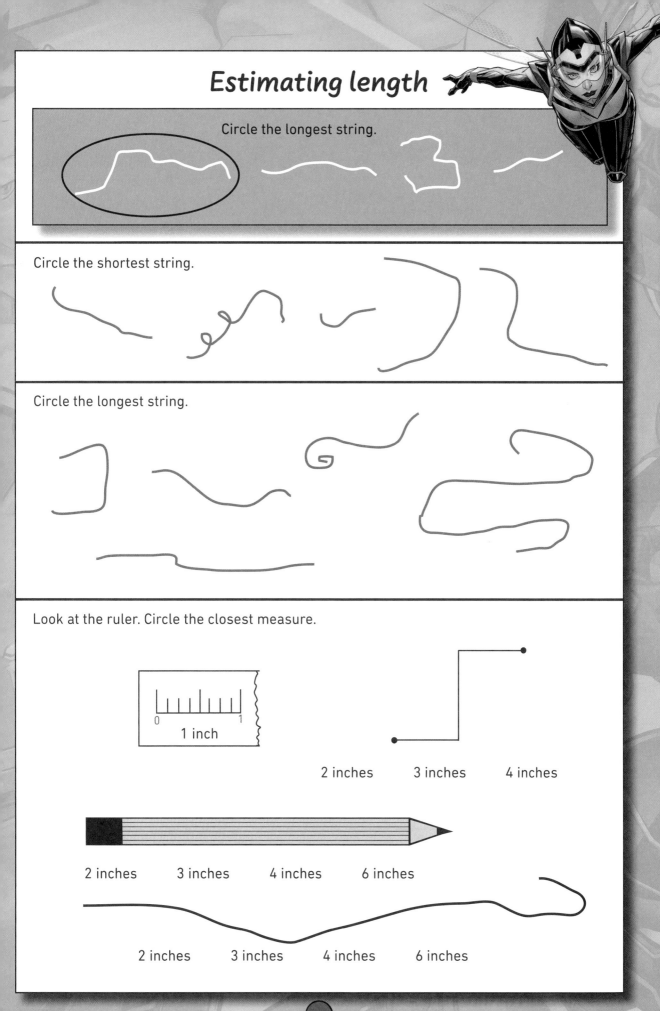

Addition properties

Circle the number that makes the sentence true.

___ + 3 = 3

(0)   3   6

25 + 41 = 41 + ___

16   66   (25)

Circle the number that makes the sentence true.

___ + 3 = 6

0   3   6

15 + ___ = 20

15   10   5

___ + 22 = 22 + 18

18   22   44

50 + 25 = 25 + ___

25   50   75

___ + 19 = 19

19   0   1

80 + 40 = 40 + ___

80   0   120

Complete the number sentences.

[ ] = 27 + 27   45 + 0 = [ ]   15 + 30 = 30 + [ ]

63 + 3 = [ ] + 63   [ ] + 0 = 6   12 + 21 = 21 + [ ]

2 + 41 = [ ] + 2   [ ] + 12 = 30   [ ] + 44 = 44 + 14

45 + [ ] = 45   [ ] + 0 = 16   200 + 800 = 800 + [ ]

[ ] + 0 = 235   18 + 0 = [ ]   333 + 123 = [ ] + 333

Add or subtract?

Write + or - in the box.

8 [-] 7 = 1   16 [-] 8 = 8   6 [+] 7 = 13

Write + or - in the box.

4 [ ] 4 = 8	7 [ ] 7 = 0	8 [ ] 6 = 2	5 [ ] 5 = 0
12 [ ] 6 = 6	10 [ ] 4 = 6	2 [ ] 8 = 10	22 [ ] 7 = 15
8 [ ] 6 = 14	12 [ ] 6 = 18	3 [ ] 6 = 9	13 [ ] 10 = 3
17 [ ] 10 = 7	14 [ ] 4 = 10	15 [ ] 5 = 10	8 [ ] 10 = 18

Write the answer in the box.

I add 8 to a number and the answer is 9.
What number did I start with?

10 added to a number gives a total of 12.
What is the number?

I take 9 from a number and have 6 left.
What number did I start with?

14 added to a number makes 28.
What is the number?

I subtract 7 from a number and the answer
is 14. What number did I start with?

Two numbers add up to 19. One of the
numbers is 8. What is the other number?

Write + or - in the box.

15 [ ] 8 = 7	20 [ ] 5 = 25	30 [ ] 30 = 0	40 [ ] 38 = 2
22 [ ] 2 = 20	24 [ ] 2 = 22	18 [ ] 12 = 30	66 [ ] 16 = 50
35 [ ] 6 = 41	60 [ ] 3 = 63	30 [ ] 26 = 56	23 [ ] 32 = 55
40 [ ] 20 = 20	34 [ ] 2 = 32	13 [ ] 14 = 27	34 [ ] 5 = 29

Subtracting

Write the answers between the lines.

739	685	788
− 221	− 202	− 345
518	483	443

Write the answers between the lines.

563	766	509	999
− 211	− 435	− 103	− 333

567	836	378	598
− 346	− 435	− 222	− 123

878	989	349	120
− 456	− 241	− 219	− 100

768	559	789	445
− 234	− 213	− 321	− 220

Write the answers between the lines.

$2.44	$8.76	$4.23	$5.51	$7.79
− $1.21	− $3.23	− $2.22	− $3.50	− $3.38

18

Working with coins

Write the answers in the boxes.

Falcon has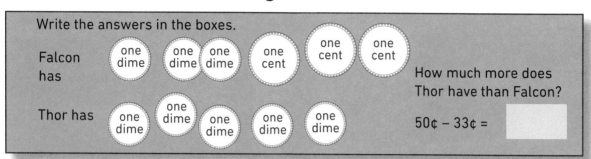

How much more does Thor have than Falcon?

Thor has

$50¢ - 33¢ =$

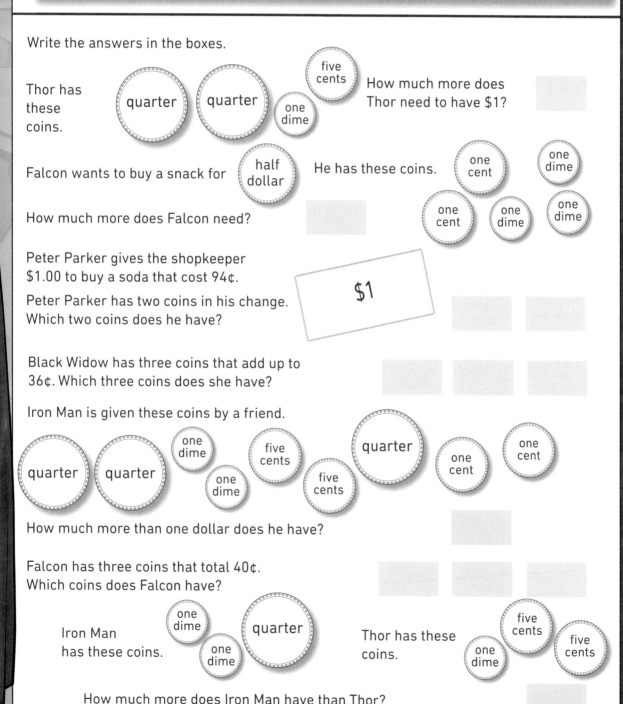

Write the answers in the boxes.

Thor has these coins.

How much more does Thor need to have $1?

Falcon wants to buy a snack for half dollar

He has these coins.

How much more does Falcon need?

Peter Parker gives the shopkeeper $1.00 to buy a soda that cost 94¢.

Peter Parker has two coins in his change. Which two coins does he have?

$1

Black Widow has three coins that add up to 36¢. Which three coins does she have?

Iron Man is given these coins by a friend.

How much more than one dollar does he have?

Falcon has three coins that total 40¢. Which coins does Falcon have?

Iron Man has these coins.

Thor has these coins.

How much more does Iron Man have than Thor?

Money problems

Look at these coins.

How much more is needed to make 75¢?   30¢

How much is 15¢ and 19¢?   34¢

Write the answers in the boxes.

What is the total of 40¢ and 50¢?

What is 70¢ less 25¢?

Hawkeye collects nickels and has 45¢ worth.
How many nickels does he have?

Doctor Strange has these coins. Which
coin does he need to make $1.00?

Thor starts out with 90¢ but loses 35¢. How much does he have left?

Captain America has four coins that add up
to 17¢. Which coins does he have?

Which four of these coins add
up to $0.86?

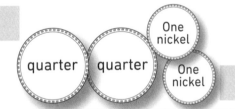

How much is four groups of coins
with 1 dime and 1 nickel in each group?

These coins are shared equally by two mutants.
How much does each mutant get?

Write the answers in the boxes.

25¢ + 25¢ =   20¢ + 26¢ =   25¢ + 7¢ =

30¢ − 20¢ =   48¢ − 8¢ =   54¢ − 14¢ =

15¢ + 55¢ =   72¢ + 13¢ =   78¢ - 28¢ =

Measurement problems

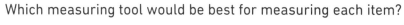

yardstick

measuring wheel

tape measure

ruler

Which measuring tool would be best to measure a garden? **measuring wheel**

Which measuring tool would be best for measuring each item?

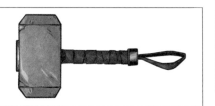

Loki's sceptre

Doctor Strange

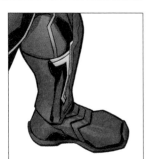

Vision's boot

Ultron's arm

Hawkeye's arrows

Round a building

Thor's hammer

The star on Captain
America's shield

Thor's cloak

Naming 2-dimensional shapes

circle   square

Write the name of each shape inside it.
Use the words in the Word Box.

Word Box

hexagon   octagon   pentagon
rectangle square   triangle

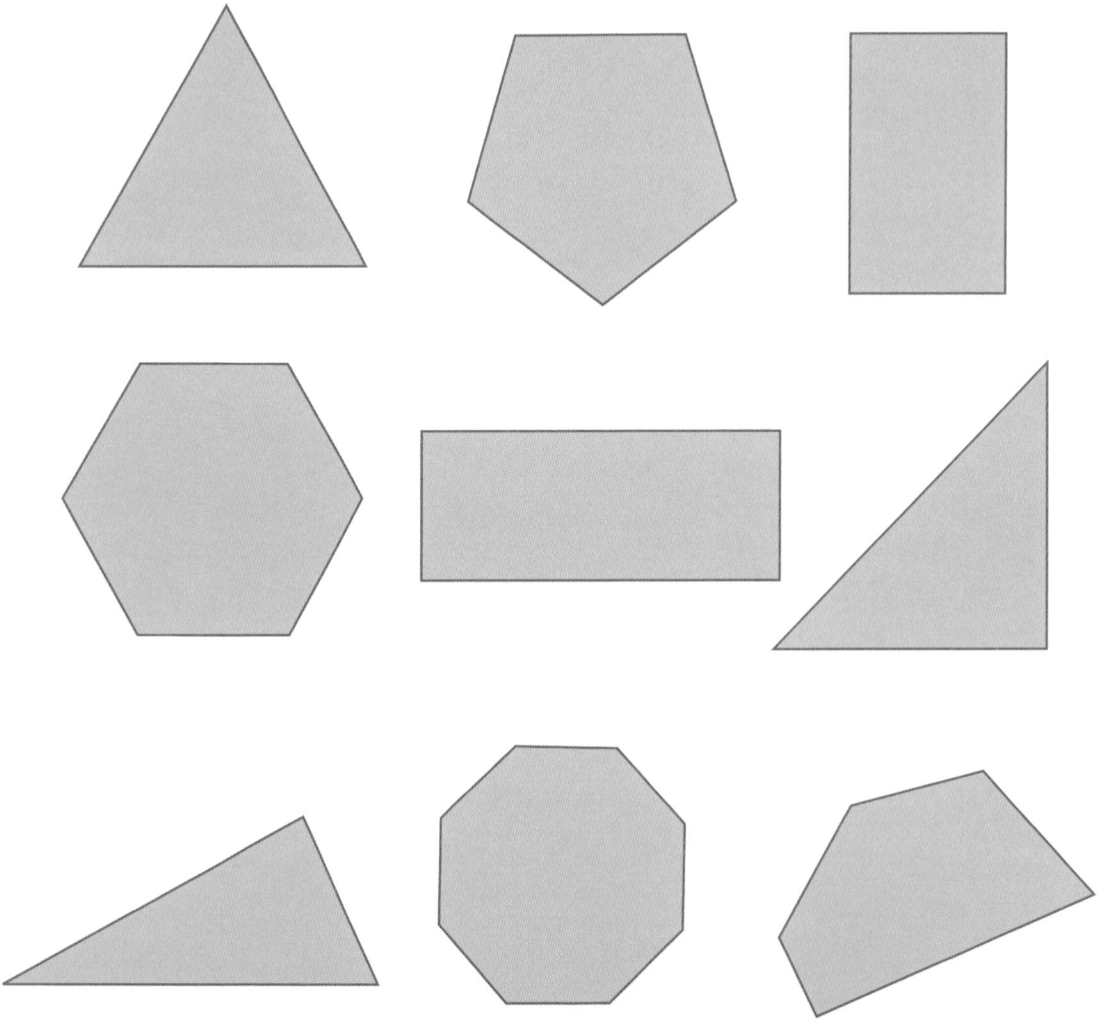

Sorting 2-dimensional shapes

square   circle   diamond

Draw the shapes with straight sides.

Find the square corners. Draw the shapes below.

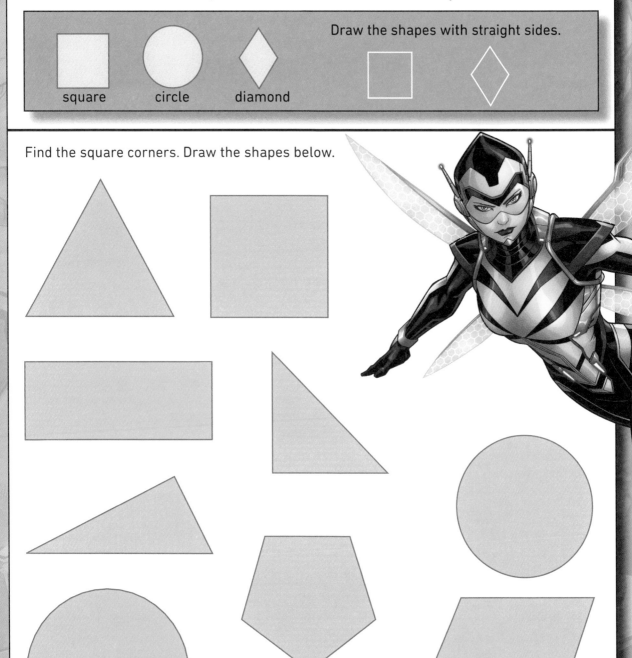

Draw the shapes with square corners.	Draw the shapes with no square corners.

Picture graphs

Look at this picture graph. Then answer the questions.

JEAN GREY'S PENS

Clear	○	○	○	○	○
Red	●	●	●		
Blue	◐	◐	◐	◐	
Yellow	◐	◐	◐		
Black	●				

How many blue pens does Jean Grey have?

4

Does Jean have more blue pens or yellow pens?

blue

How many pens does Jean have in all?

16

Look at this picture graph. Then answer the questions.

BOOKS ON DOCTOR STRANGE'S SHELF

Art	📗	📗	📗		
Comics	📗				
History	📘	📘	📘	📘	
Science	📗	📗	📗	📗	📗
Sports	📗	📗	📗		

How many science books does the doctor have?

Does he have more books about art than history?

How many more science books does he have than books about sports?

How many comic books and history books does Doctor Strange have?

Look at this picture graph. Then answer the questions.

NUMBER OF TIMES CHARACTERS WERE SEEN IN TIMES SQUARE

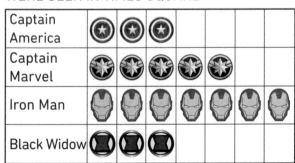

Captain America	★	★	★				
Captain Marvel	★	★	★	★	★		
Iron Man	▢	▢	▢	▢	▢	▢	▢
Black Widow	◉	◉	◉				

Which character was seen most times in Times Square?

How many more times was Captain Marvel seen than Black Widow?

How many more times was Iron Man seen than Captain America?

How many times were the characters seen in all?

Equations

Circle the correct number sentence.

7 + 3 = 10   (4 + 3 = 7)   4 − 3 = 1 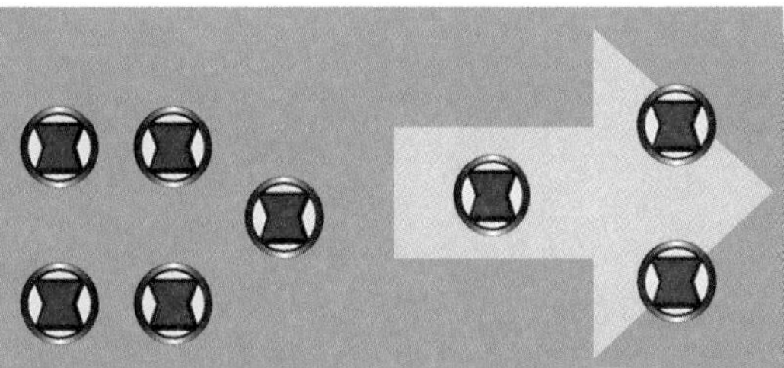   2 + 4 = 6   2 + 3 = 5   (5 − 3 = 2)

Circle the correct addition sentence.

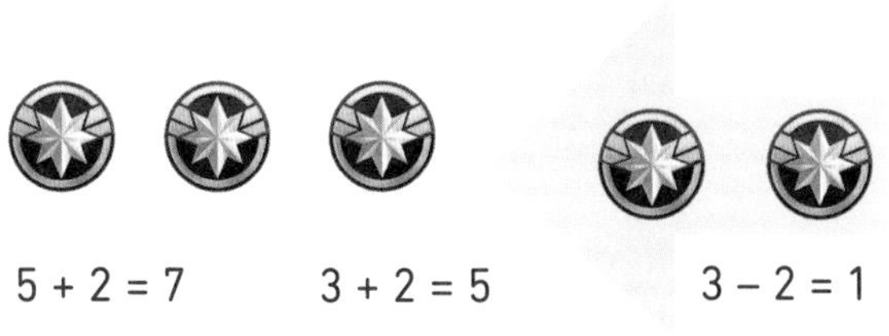

5 + 2 = 7   3 + 2 = 5   3 − 2 = 1    4 + 2 = 6   5 − 1 = 4   5 + 1 = 6

Circle the correct subtraction sentence.

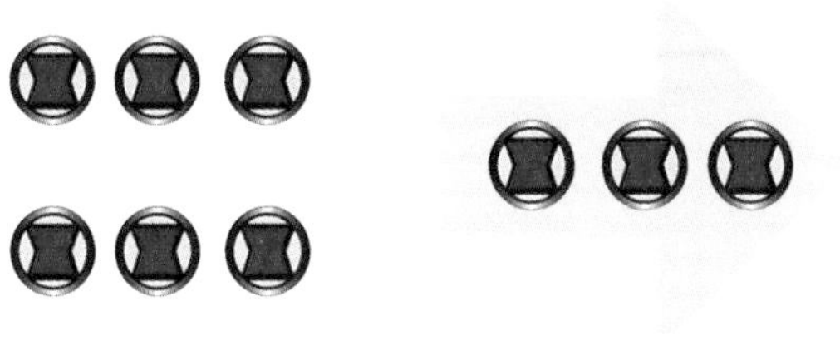

3 + 3 = 6   3 − 3 = 0   6 − 3 = 3 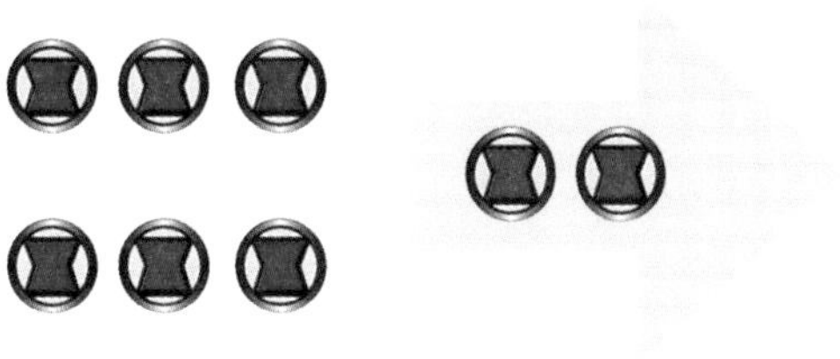   6 − 2 = 4   6 + 2 = 8   4 − 2 = 2

Circle the correct number sentence.

9 − 3 = 6   5 − 3 = 2   6 − 3 = 3    5 − 2 = 3   2 + 5 = 7   7 − 5 = 2

6 − 4 = 2   4 + 2 = 6   6 + 2 = 8    5 − 1 = 4   4 + 5 = 9   9 − 4 = 5

Location on grid

Look at the grid and then answer the question.

Which box is Spider-Man in?

B, 1

2

1

A   B

Look at the grid and then answer the question below.

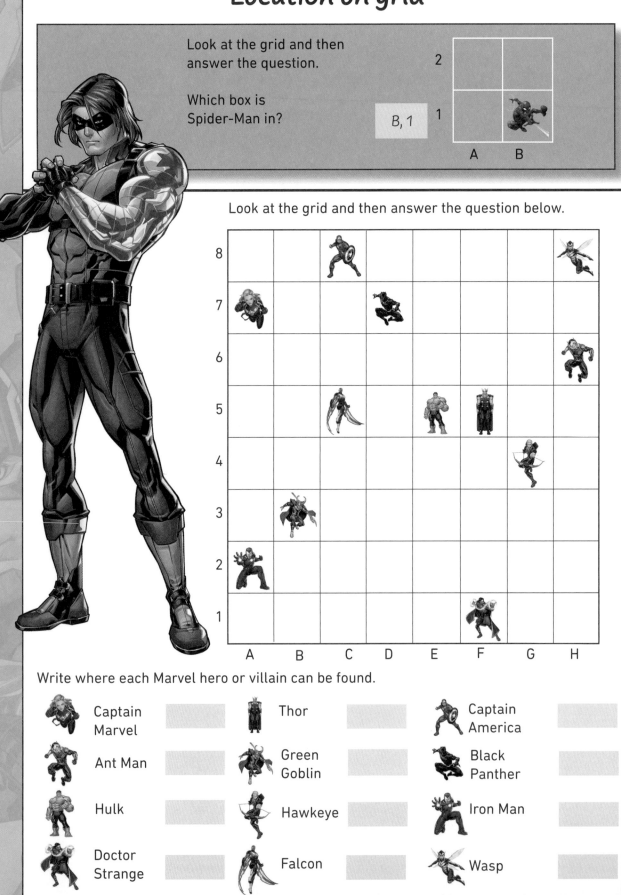

Write where each Marvel hero or villain can be found.

	Captain Marvel			Thor			Captain America	
Ant Man				Green Goblin			Black Panther	
Hulk				Hawkeye			Iron Man	
Doctor Strange				Falcon			Wasp	

26

Placing on grid

Draw a ✳ in B, 2

2		✳
1		
	A	B

Look at the grid and then answer the question below.

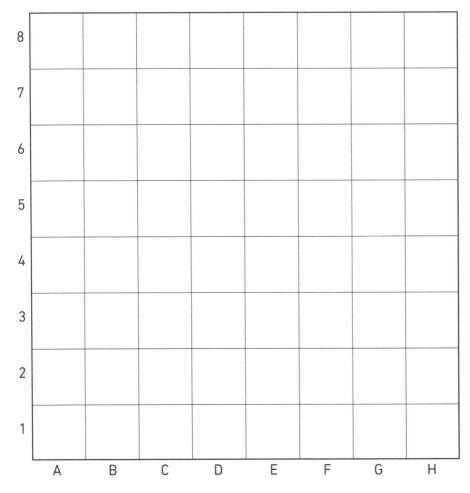

Draw each picture in the correct box on the grid.

△ in B, 4　　◯ in H, 7　　▲ in D, 5　　▬ in A, 6

▢ in C, 3　　◻ in E, 8　　■ in F, 2　　◉ in G, 1

◎ in B, 7　　◡ in H, 4　　● in D, 8　　◡ in A, 2

Counting by 3s, 4s, and 5s

Find the pattern. Continue each row.

Count by 3s.	12	15	18	21	24	27	30
Count by 4s.	36	32	28	24	20	16	12
Count by 5s.	35	40	45	50	55	60	65

Find the pattern. Continue each row.

9	12	15					30
0	4	8					
25	30	35					
71	74	77					
76	72	68					
70	75	80					
14	17	20					
21	18	15					
35	30	25					
84	80	76					56
22	27	32					
29	33	37					
44	39	34					
77	80	83					
100							70

Adding

Write the answer between the lines.

200	320	325
+ 200	+ 226	+ 324
400	546	649

Write the answer between the lines.

700	400	200	200	600
+ 200	+ 400	+ 400	+ 300	+ 100

440	320	660	460	260
+ 220	+ 430	+ 330	+ 220	+ 230

376	566	464	701	324
+ 223	+ 333	+ 234	+ 108	+ 601

484	221	407	417	105
+ 101	+ 261	+ 370	+ 280	+ 802

$4.42	$3.07	$4.40	$3.09	$3.20
+ $0.22	+ $2.21	+ $2.35	+ $2.50	+ $3.25

29

Comparing and ordering

Write these numbers in order, starting with the smallest.

| 431 | 678 | 273 | 586 | 273 | 431 | 586 | 678 |

Write these numbers in order,
starting with the smallest.

876	245	374	740				
748	387	123	267				
349	338	298	309				
387	972	836	487				
879	341	342	897				
298	973	242	556				
874	478	847	748				
237	327	273	372				
209	204	323	342				
342	243	434	234				
24	23	42	98				
502	52	250	520				
657	576	764	234				
309	903	93	39				
667	676	766	666				

Comparing and ordering

Circle the numbers that are greater than 200.

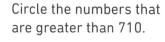

99
232
201
211
199

Circle the numbers that are greater than 710.

799
711
777
709
700

Circle the numbers that are less than 550.

600   500   507
550
528

Circle the numbers that are between 490 and 510.

480   520
511
505   499

Circle the amounts that are greater than $1.00.

99¢ $0.85
$1.08
105¢ $1.99

Circle the amounts that are less than $2.50.

$1.99
251¢ $2.48 $2.55   245¢

Circle the amounts that are between $1.85 and $2.00.

167¢
186¢
195¢ $3.00
$1.83

Missing addends

Write the missing addend.

6 + **7** = 13

Write the missing addend.

2 + ___ = 8

5 + ___ = 11

8 + ___ = 10

8 + ___ = 14

Write the missing addend.

4 + ___ = 8	6 + ___ = 15	6 + ___ = 9	5 + ___ = 11
2 + ___ = 7	2 + ___ = 10	5 + ___ = 12	3 + ___ = 8
7 + ___ = 14	3 + ___ = 9	3 + ___ = 6	8 + ___ = 12
8 + ___ = 11	3 + ___ = 10	6 + ___ = 11	1 + ___ = 2
6 + ___ = 12	5 + ___ = 6	3 + ___ = 4	8 + ___ = 12
8 + ___ = 16	8 + ___ = 17	2 + ___ = 5	3 + ___ = 7
4 + ___ = 6	4 + ___ = 13	5 + ___ = 13	7 + ___ = 16
6 + ___ = 13	8 + ___ = 14	5 + ___ = 14	7 + ___ = 15
9 + ___ = 18	7 + ___ = 15	4 + ___ = 10	2 + ___ = 3

Reading tables

Read the table. Then answer the questions.

FAVORITE SUPER HEROES

Black Widow	51
Iron Man	76
Thor	87
Spider-Man	55
Black Panther	76

Who is the favorite?

Who is the least favorite?

Who are the joint second favorites?

Read the table. Then answer the questions.

FAVORITE VILLAINS

Venom	6
Doc Ock	2
Green Goblin	11
Thanos	3
Loki	9

How many people chose Venom?

Which crook did 2 people choose?

How many more people like Loki than Venom?

Did more people choose Green Goblin or Thanos?

Read the table. Then answer the questions.

WEIGHT OF SUPER HEROES

NAME	Thor	Hulk	Spider-Man	Black Panther	Hawkeye
POUNDS	640	1,200	167	201	230

Which Super Hero weighs more than 1,000 pounds?

Which Super Hero weighs less than 200 pounds?

How much more does Hawkeye weigh than Black Panther?

How much less does Thor weigh than Hulk?

Extending geometric patterns

Circle the next three squares in each pattern.

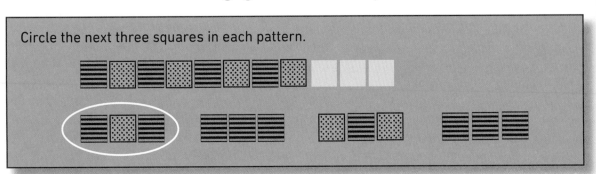

Circle the next square in each pattern.

Circle the next two squares in each pattern.

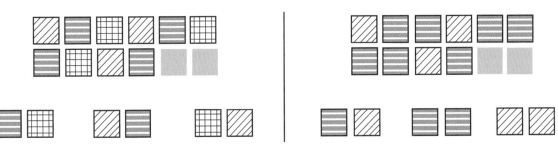

Circle the next three squares in each pattern.

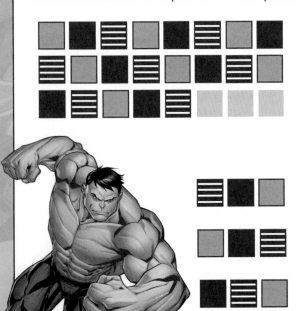

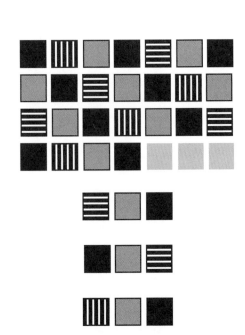

34

Adding

Write the answer in each box.

22 + 18 + 11 = [51]   18 + 12 + 20 = [50]

Write the answer in each box.

22 + 35 + 20 =

42 + 20 + 10 =

33 + 22 + 23 =

22 + 20 + 40 =

12 + 13 + 18 =

15 + 21 + 32 =

31 + 22 + 16 =

52 + 18 + 12 =

40 + 30 + 10 =

28 + 11 + 60 =

22 + 23 + 24 =

14 + 24 + 34 =

60 + 15 + 15 =

15 + 15 + 15 =

13 + 19 + 20 =

23 + 10 + 7 =

10 + 15 + 9 =

35 + 35 + 7 =

22 + 23 + 14 =

15 + 21 + 22 =

30 + 40 + 20 =

15 + 46 + 23 =

13 + 70 + 11 =

24 + 25 + 50 =

16 + 10 + 30 =

13 + 12 + 15 =

13 + 14 + 15 =

15 + 15 + 60 =

12 + 34 + 44 =

20 + 24 + 15 =

35 + 45 + 9 =

21 + 21 + 16 =

10 + 20 + 60 =

23 + 34 + 16 =

11 + 14 + 50 =

31 + 38 + 20 =

Write the answer in each box.

5 + 6 + 7 + 8 =

3 + 5 + 7 + 9 =

2 + 4 + 6 + 8 =

3 + 6 + 6 + 3 =

2 + 2 + 5 + 7 =

5 + 8 + 9 + 2 =

8 + 7 + 8 + 9 =

4 + 9 + 9 + 8 =

Adding

Write the answer in the box.

34	26	73
+ 13	+ 15	+ 27
47	41	100

Write the answer in the box. Regroup if needed.

22	43	53	52
+ 13	+ 23	+ 26	+ 16

37	72	32	45
+ 20	+ 23	+ 28	+ 24

50	31	28	50
+ 28	+ 9	+ 17	+ 45

56	28	61	51
+ 16	+ 38	+ 16	+ 13

39	74	53	43
+ 39	+ 12	+ 28	+ 12

28	44	29	56
+ 13	+ 28	+ 16	+ 17

23	33	23	55
+ 29	+ 12	+ 57	+ 15

29	37	85	28
+ 24	+ 27	+ 14	+ 23

46	38	27	26
+ 54	+ 50	+ 37	+ 19

Subtracting

Write the answer in the box.

54 – 12 = 42   51 – 21 = 30

Write the answer in the box.

33 – 16 =   46 – 12 =   55 – 31 =   58 – 32 =

76 – 31 =   48 – 23 =   66 – 21 =   73 – 25 =

62 – 33 =   71 – 28 =   45 – 35 =   79 – 33 =

48 – 25 =   66 – 16 =   36 – 13 =   99 – 90 =

67 – 27 =   55 – 36 =   68 – 23 =   59 – 51 =

Write the answer in the box.

34¢ – 24¢ =   46¢ – 21¢ =   55¢ – 44¢ =   67¢ – 43¢ =

24¢ – 18¢ =   74¢ – 31¢ =   88¢ – 34¢ =   99¢ – 22¢ =

33¢ – 23¢ =   66¢ – 24¢ =   77¢ – 41¢ =   35¢ – 31¢ =

64¢ – 25¢ =   48¢ – 33¢ =   56¢ – 34¢ =   44¢ – 27¢ =

45¢ – 23¢ =   74¢ – 24¢ =   57¢ – 16¢ =   12¢ – 4¢ =

Write the answer in the box.

How much is 90¢ minus 35¢?

Take 56¢ away from $1.00.

How much is 95¢ minus 44¢?

Take away 87¢ from 99¢.

What is the difference between 56¢ and $1.21?

How much less than 98 in. is 22 in.?

The Black Widow has 45¢. She spends 30¢ on candy. How much does she have left?

Take away 58 in. from 90 in.

Multiplication as repeated addition

Write how many.

There are 3 groups.

There are 2 in each group.

You can add.

2 + 2 + 2 = 6

You can multiply.

3 twos = 6 and 3 x 2 = 6

Write how many.

2 + 2 + 2 + 2 = ☐

4 twos = ☐

☐ + ☐ = ☐

☐ twos = ☐

☐ + ☐ + ☐ + ☐ + ☐ = ☐

☐ twos = ☐

3 + 3 = ☐

2 threes = ☐

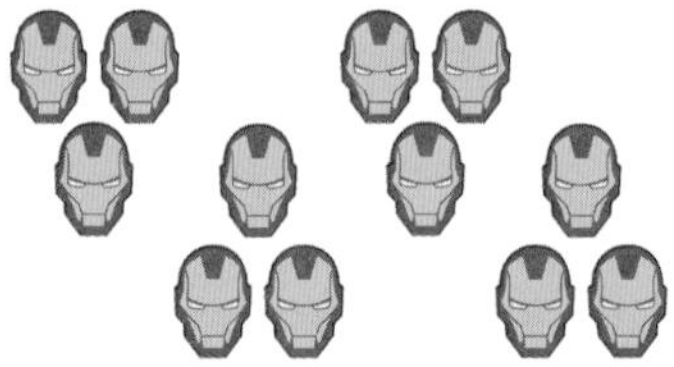

☐ + ☐ + ☐ + ☐ = ☐

☐ threes = ☐

☐ + ☐ + ☐ = ☐

☐ threes = ☐

Write how many.

How many groups? ☐

How many in each group? ☐

Write as addition.

☐ + ☐ + ☐ = ☐

Write as multiplication.

☐ x ☐ = ☐

How many groups? ☐

How many in each group? ☐

Write as addition.

☐ + ☐ + ☐ + ☐ = ☐

Write as multiplication.

☐ x ☐ = ☐

Choose the operation

Put either + or - in the box to make each answer correct.

13 $+$ 13 = 26   24 $-$ 14 = 10   28 $+$ 12 = 40

Put either + or - in the box to make each answer correct.

30 ☐ 19 = 49   21 ☐ 8 = 13   18 ☐ 11 = 7   29 ☐ 23 = 52

40 ☐ 25 = 15   34 ☐ 16 = 50   65 ☐ 25 = 40   22 ☐ 32 = 54

19 ☐ 17 = 36   45 ☐ 13 = 32   48 ☐ 12 = 36   47 ☐ 12 = 59

45 ☐ 20 = 25   79 ☐ 22 = 57   84 ☐ 32 = 52   16 ☐ 16 = 32

45 ☐ 45 = 0   45 ☐ 45 = 90   39 ☐ 54 = 93   73 ☐ 34 = 39

Write the answer in the box.

I add 13 to a number and the answer is 50. What number did I start with? ☐

67 added to a number makes 80. What is the number? ☐

45 added to a number gives a total of 64. What is the number? ☐

I subtract 35 from a number and the result is 24. What number did I start with? ☐

I take 22 away from a number and have 15 left. What number did I start with? ☐

Two numbers add up to 55. One of the numbers is 11. What is the other number? ☐

Two numbers are added together and the total is 45. One of the numbers is 22. What is the other number? ☐

After spending 45¢, I have 50¢ left. How much did I start with? ☐

Write + or – in the box.

17¢ ☐ 25¢ = 42¢   34¢ ☐ 17¢ = 19¢   82¢ ☐ 41¢ = 41¢

65¢ ☐ 65¢ = 0¢   25¢ ☐ 13¢ = 12¢   60¢ ☐ 46¢ = 14¢

54¢ ☐ 18¢ = 72¢   28¢ ☐ 24¢ = 52¢   54¢ ☐ 7¢ = 37¢

43¢ ☐ 23¢ = 66¢   63¢ ☐ 37¢ = 26¢   45¢ ☐ 23¢ = 68¢

Venn diagrams

Read the clues to find the secret number.

4 5 6 7 8

3
5 7

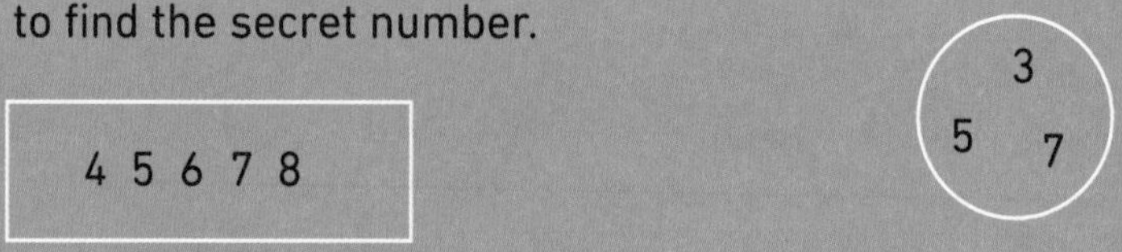

It is in both the rectangle and the circle.

It is greater than 5.

What number is it? 7

Read the clues to find the secret number.

10
12 13
16 14

12 15
11 14
13

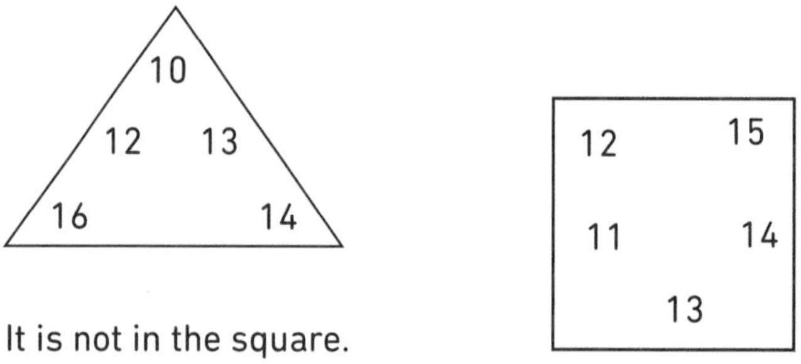

It is not in the square.
It is an even number.
It is less than 12.

What number is it?

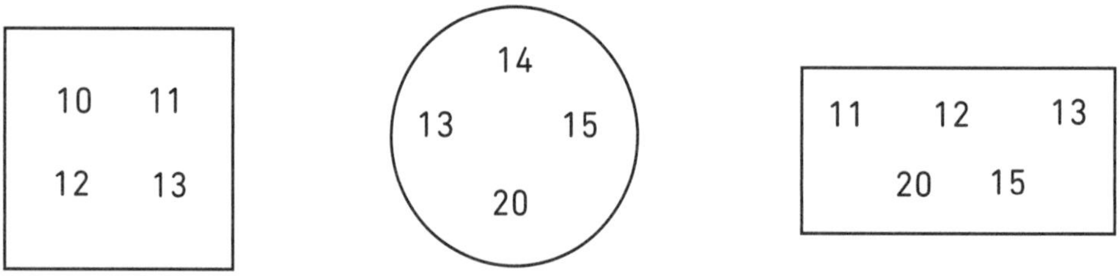

10 11
12 13

14
13 15
20

11 12 13
20 15

It is in the rectangle and the circle.
It is greater than 13 and less than 20.
It is an odd number.

What number is it?

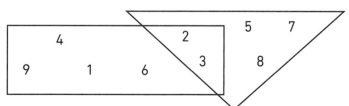

4
9 1 6

2
3

5 7
8

It is not an even number.
It is in the triangle.
It is in the rectangle.

What number is it?

Working with coins

Black Widow has these coins:

How much more does she need to have $1.00?

20¢

Black Widow has these coins:

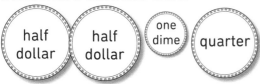

How much does Black Widow have altogether?

Captain America has three coins that total 51¢. Which coins does he have?

Captain Marvel has three coins. They add up to 65¢. Which coins does she have?

How much less than $1.00 is the total of these coins?

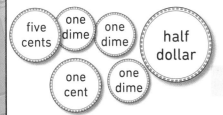

Which coin is smaller in size than a penny?

What is the total of these coins?

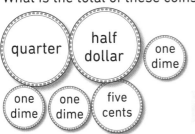

Spider-Man has these coins:

Thor has these coins:

How much more money does Spider-Man have than Thor?

Which three coins add up to 36¢?

Iron Man has 68¢. Which 3 coins could he be given to make his money total 80¢?

Hawkeye has these coins:

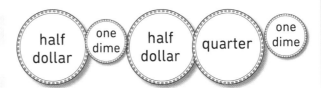

Black Panther has these coins:

How much more does Hawkeye have than Black Panther?

Money problems

Write the answer in the box.

How many dimes are needed to make a total of 50¢?

One dollar is shared equally by five children. How much will they each get?

How much do three dimes make?

How many groups of $2.00 are needed to make $8.00?

Thor spends $1.25 and gives the storekeeper $2.00. How much change does he get?

After spending $1.50, Nick Fury has 90¢ left. How much did Nick Fury start with?

How many 25¢ coins are equal to $2.25?

Captain Marvel has $3.60 and is given $6.40. How much does she have now?

Hulk needs $8.00 for a T-shirt but only has $1.50. How much more does Hulk need?

Peter Parker has $5.55 but needs $9.00 to buy a notebook. How much more money does Peter need?

Write the answer in the box.

$1.00 − $0.60 =

$3.20 − $1.90 =

34¢ − 15¢ =

56¢ + 76¢ =

$3.40 − $0.75 =

$2.50 + $2.50 =

$6.00 + $5.25 =

$4.67 + $3.65 =

70¢ − 23¢ =

$4.50 − $0.70 =

$2.30 + $0.99 =

75¢ − 45¢ =

86¢ − 40¢ =

$6.50 + $4.00 =

$4.50 + $5.35 =

Measurement problems

Write the answer in the box.

How many grams are equal to 1 kilogram? | 1,000 g

How many milliliters are the same as 1 liter? | 1,000 ml

Write the answer in the box. Use the information above.

How many grams are equal to 4 kilograms?

How many grams are the same as 0.7 kilograms?

How many milliliters are the same as 3 liters?

How many 250 ml glasses are equal to one liter?

Is 800 ml more or less than half a liter?

How many milliliters are the same as 0.5 liters?

How many 100 g weights are equal to 1 kilogram?

How many grams are the same as 2.5 kg?

Is 400 ml more or less than half a liter?

How many 300 ml jars are equal to 1.2 liters?

Which unit of measurement would you use for each of these?
Choose from meter, milligram, milliliter, liter, kilometer, and kilogram.

To measure the mass of Hulk.

To measure the capacity of a bathtub.

To measure the capacity of a spoon.

To measure the mass of a spider.

To measure the distance from Chicago to Detroit.

To measure the length of an airplane.

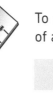

43

2-dimensional shapes

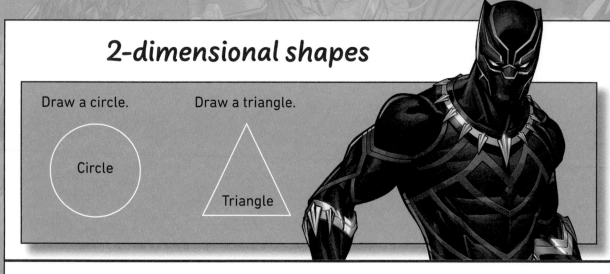

Draw a circle.

Circle

Draw a triangle.

Triangle

Draw each shape in the box.

Rectangle	Circle	Square

Pentagon	Hexagon	Octagon

Triangle with three equal sides	Triangle with two equal sides	Triangle with no equal sides

Properties of polygons

Circle the polygon that has the same number of sides as the rectangle.

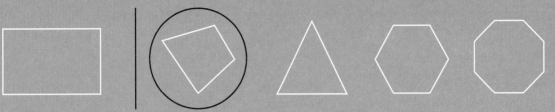

Circle the polygon that has the same number of sides as the first shape.

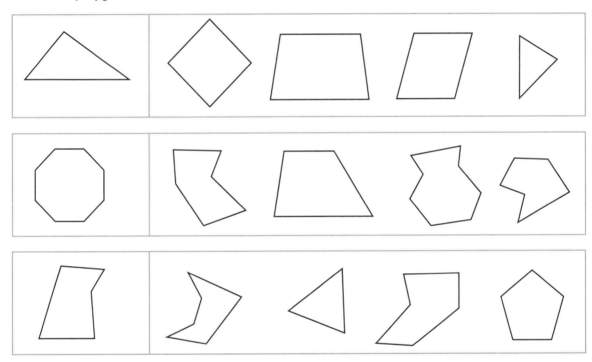

Circle the polygon that has a different number of sides.

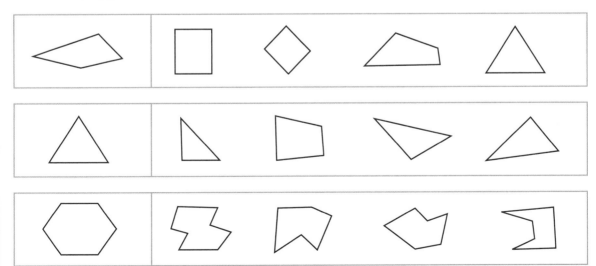

Pictographs

Look at this pictograph. Then answer the questions.

PEOPLE SAVED BY THOR

Monday	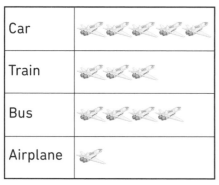
Tuesday	
Wednesday	
Thursday	
Friday	

Thor can save six people at a time

⚒ = 6 people

How many people did Thor save on Friday?

12

Were more people saved on Wednesday or Monday?

Wednesday

How many more people were saved on Thursday than Friday?

12

How many people did Thor save on Monday and Tuesday?

36

Look at this pictograph. Then answer the questions.

FAVORITE WAY OF TRAVELING

Car	
Train	
Bus	
Airplane	

✈ = 4 people

How many people like to travel by bus?

Do more people like to travel by bus or by airplane?

Which way to travel did the least people choose?

How many more people like to travel by car than by train?

How many people chose train and bus?

How many people were included in the pictograph?

Look at this pictograph. Then answer the questions.

NUMBER OF CRIMINALS CAUGHT

Captain America	
Hulk	
Iron Man	
Thor	

each badge stands for 10 people

Who caught the most criminals?

Who caught the fewest criminals?

How many more criminals did Iron Man catch than Hulk?

How many criminals did Captain America and Thor catch altogether?

How many were caught in total?

Most likely/least likely

Look at the pictures. Then answer the questions.

Which badge would you be least likely to pick without looking?

Which badge would you be most likely to pick without looking?

Look at the spinner. Then answer the questions.

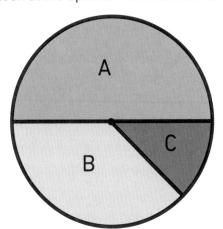

Is the spinner more likely to land on A or B?

Is the spinner more likely to land on B or C?

Which letter is the spinner most likely to land on?

Which letter is the spinner least likely to land on?

Look at the tally chart. Then answer the questions.

Imagine that each time you shake the bag, one coin falls out.

TALLY OF COINS IN THE BAG	
COLOR	TALLIES
Quarters	llll
Nickels	ll
Dimes	llll lll
Pennies	llll

Is a penny or a dime more likely to fall out?

Is a quarter or a nickel more likely to fall out?

Which coin is most likely to fall out?

Which coin is least likely to fall out?

Square corners

Circle the square corners on all these shapes.

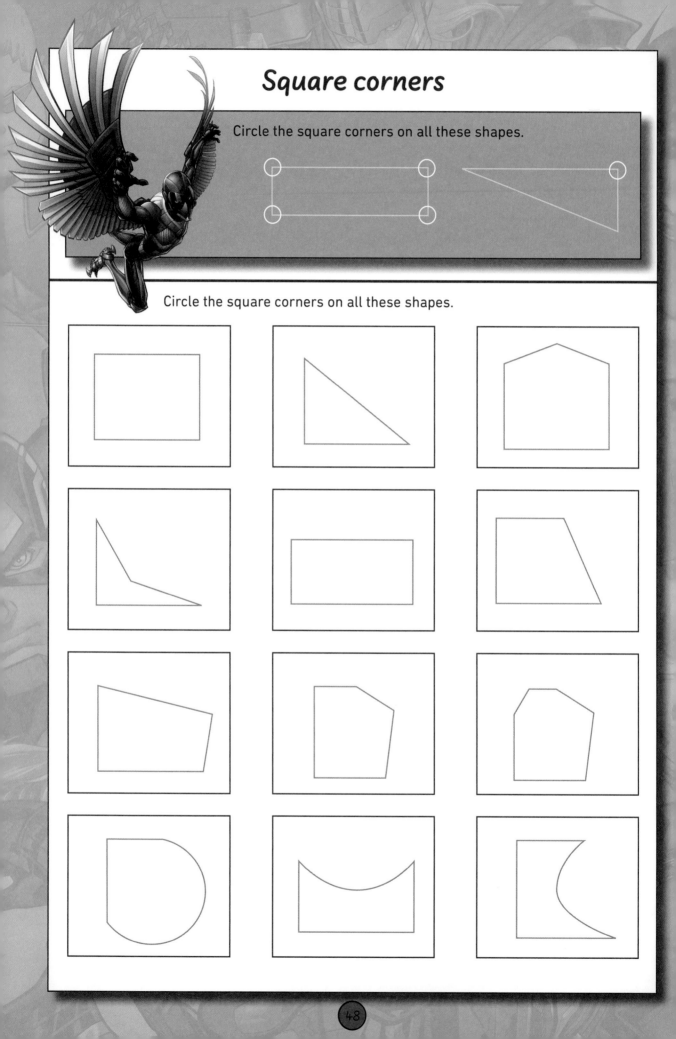

Circle the square corners on all these shapes.

48

Square corners

Circle the square corners on all these shapes.

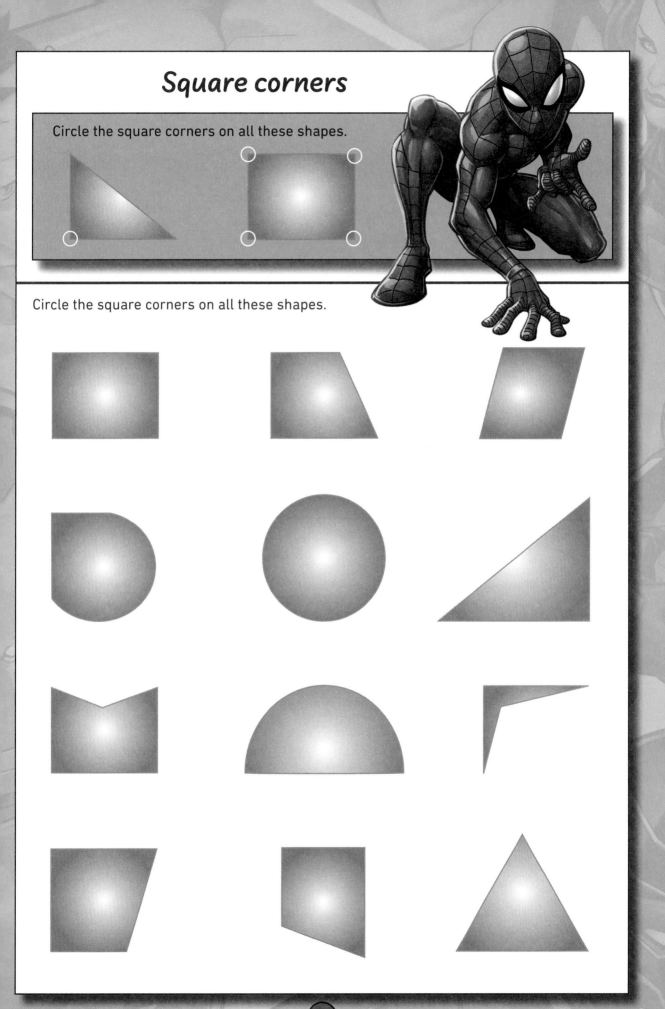

Circle the square corners on all these shapes.

Place value

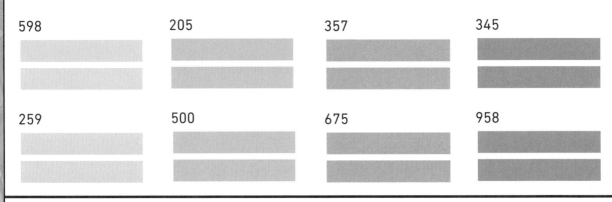

The value of 5 in 5̲23 is | 500 | or | five hundred
The value of 5 in 25̲3 is | 50 | or | fifty
The value of 5 in 235̲ is | 5 | or | five

Change the 3 in 38 to 4. | 48 | The number is greater by | 10

What is the value of 5 in these numbers?

598

205

357

345

259

500

675

958

Circle each number that has a 7 with the value of seventy.

279　　　　748　　　　897　　　　171　　　　972　　　　737

Circle each number that has a 3 with the value of three hundred.

324　　　　293　　　　388　　　　930　　　　663　　　　375

Circle each number that has an 8 with the value of eight.

608　　　　883　　　　786　　　　283　　　　198　　　　678

Write the new number. Then write the value.

Change the 7 in 76 to 9. 　　　The number is greater by

Change the 4 in 84 to 9. 　　　The number is greater by

Change the 3 in 341 to 4. 　　　The number is greater by

Change the 8 in 282 to 7. 　　　The number is less by

Change the 5 in 205 to 2. 　　　The number is less by

Change the 7 in 107 to 3. 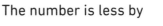　　　The number is less by

Fractions of shapes

Shade half of each shape.

Shade half of each shape.

Shade one-third of each shape.

51

Finding patterns

Figure out the pattern. Write the missing numbers.

2	4	6	8	10	12	14	16	18	20

Find the counting pattern. Write the missing numbers.

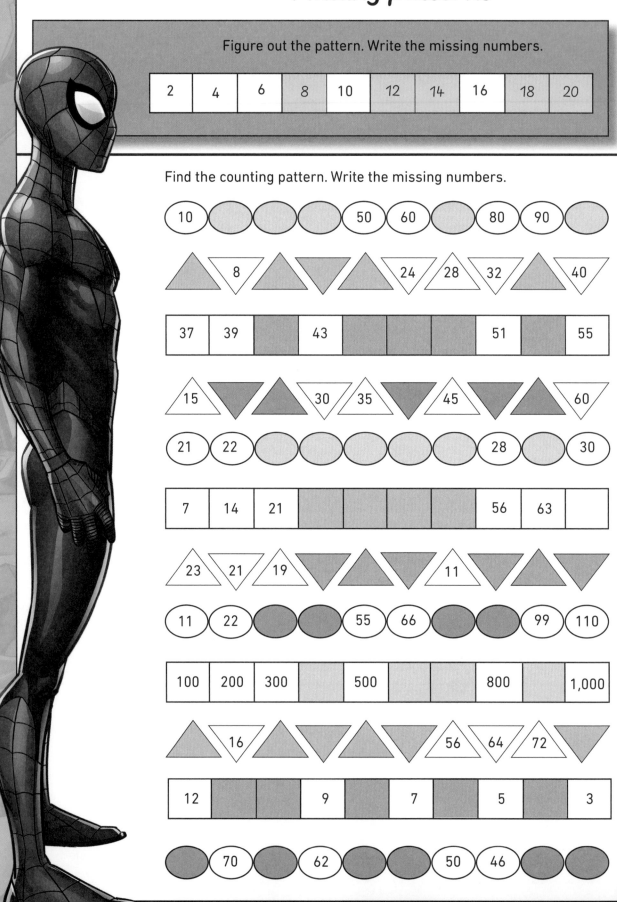

10   50   60   80   90

8   24   28   32   40

| 37 | 39 | | 43 | | | | 51 | | 55 |

15   30   35   45   60

21   22   28   30

| 7 | 14 | 21 | | | | 56 | 63 | |

23   21   19   11

11   22   55   66   99   110

| 100 | 200 | 300 | | 500 | | | 800 | | 1,000 |

16   56   64   72

| 12 | | | 9 | | 7 | | 5 | | 3 |

70   62   50   46

52

Adding

Write the answer in the box.

Peter Parker has 42¢ and finds another 22¢. How much does he have in all?

Hulk has 33¢ and Iron Man has 29¢. How much do they have altogether?

Nick Fury captures 34 criminals and Captain Marvel captures 34 criminals. How many criminals did they catch together?

Tony Stark finds 12¢ in one pocket and 75¢ in his other pocket. How much does he have altogether?

A line is 23 inches long. Peter Parker adds another 25 inches to the line. How long is the line now?

What is the total when 8 is added to 38?

Three spies add their money together. They have $22, $12, and $28. How much do the spies have altogether?

A pencil 10 cm long is put end to end with another pencil 12 cm long. What is the total length of the two pencils?

What is the total when 66 is added to 16?

What is the total when 47 is added to 48?

One of Iron Man's safes contains 12 bars of gold. A second safe contains 18 bars of gold. How many bars are there altogether?

Thor spends 99¢ on a comic and then 38¢ on candy. How much does he spend altogether?

Black Widow has 2 Widow Gauntlets in her bag and 58 at home. How many Gauntlets does she have altogether?

A solar system contains 40 icy planets and 20 gassy planets. How many planets are in the system altogether?

There are 34 S.H.I.E.L.D agents in one helicopter and 36 agents in another. How many agents are there in total?

Adding

Write the answer in the box.

Nick Fury has three piles of eye patches. There are 12 eye patches in one pile, 14 in the second pile, and 18 in the third pile. How many eye patches does Nick Fury have altogether?

44

Write the answer in the box.

What is the total of 23, 13, and 3?

Black Widow is given $100 by Captain Marvel, $25 by Black Panther, and $35 by Thor. How much is she given in all?

What is the sum of 87 and 33?

How much do these coins add up to: 25¢, 50¢, 10¢, and 5¢?

Add together 40¢, 30¢, and 50¢.

What is the sum of 23, 24, and 25?

The Hulk has three pockets. One has $2.40, the second has $0.90, and the third has $2.70. How much does the Hulk have altogether?

How much is 60¢ plus 20¢ plus 10¢?

One planet has 19 moons, the second has 40 moons, and the third planet has 8 moons. How many moons are there in total?

Doctor Strange collects books. He has 299 and buys 74 more. How many books does Doctor Strange have now?

Hawkeye buys three bars of candy. One costs 30¢, the second costs 28¢, and the third costs 32¢. What is the total cost of the candy?

What is the total of 70, 80, and 90?

Three boxes of equipment are delivered to Avengers Tower. They weigh 90 lb, 90 lb, and 200 lb. How much do they weigh altogether?

Add together 12 and 36.

Captain America saves 23 children on Monday, 3 on Tuesday, and 14 on Wednesday. How many has he saved altogether?

Subtracting

Write the answer in the box.

The Wasp had 40 marbles but then lost half of them in a game. How many marbles does The Wasp have left?

20

Write the answer in the box.

I have 48 jelly beans. Then I eat 24. How many are left?

Two numbers add up to 40. One of the numbers is 28. What is the other number?

Thor's hammer is 120 inches long. A section 12 inches long is cut off. How long is Thor's hammer now?

Two numbers add up to 80. One of the numbers is 45. What is the other number?

A class has 30 children. There are 15 boys. How many of the class are girls?

Out of 46 squirrels, 38 are gray and the rest are red. How many squirrels are red?

What is 17 less than 100?

A bag contains 89 cherries. There are 14 rotten cherries in the bag. How many of the cherries are not rotten?

Two numbers total 55. One of the numbers is 32. What is the other number?

A number added to 12 makes a total of 24. What number has been added?

Ant-Man goes shopping with $10.00. He spends $1.80. How much does Ant-Man have left?

The Wasp goes shopping with $5.00. She returns home with $2.30. How much has The Wasp spent?

The sum of two numbers is 40. One of the numbers is 39. What is the other number?

Loki has $5.00 to spend. He gives $1.50 to a friend. How much does Loki have left?

Money problems

Falcon goes shopping with a five dollar bill. He spends $2.75. How much does Falcon have left?

$2.25

Captain Marvel has three bills. The total value of the bills is $35. Which bills does she have?

The Wasp has a $5 bill and a 50¢ coin. How much more does she need to have $10.00?

After spending $6.60, Black Panther still has $2.35 left. How much did Black Panther start with?

A packet of cards costs $3.95. If Hawkeye pays for them with a $5 bill, how much change will he get?

Ant-Man buys a takeaway meal that costs $8.90. He pays for his order with a $10 bill. How much change will he get?

Three newspapers cost a total of $6.25. Tony Stark pays for the newspapers with a $5 bill and two $1 bills. How much change will he get?

Apples cost 90¢ for a pound. How much will 4 pounds of apples cost?

How much change will you get if you buy books for $6.68 and pay for them with a $10 bill?

Phoenix saves 80¢ a week for 12 weeks. How much does she have after the 12 weeks?

Peter Parker buys a new microscope for $39.50 and pays for it with a $50 bill. How much change will Peter get?

The Hulk is given $2.20 in change. If he bought a shirt for $8.50, how much had he given the clerk?

How much change will you get from $20.00 if a hat costs $14.99?

The change from $5.00 is $1.20. How much was spent?

After spending $4.40 on food, Thor is given $5.60 in change. How much had Thor given to the storekeeper?

A box of chocolates costs $5.48. It is paid for with a $5 bill and a $1 bill. How much extra has been paid?

56

Measurement problems

Write the measurement shown by the arrow.

cm

1   2   3   4   5

3 cm

Write the measurement shown by the arrow.

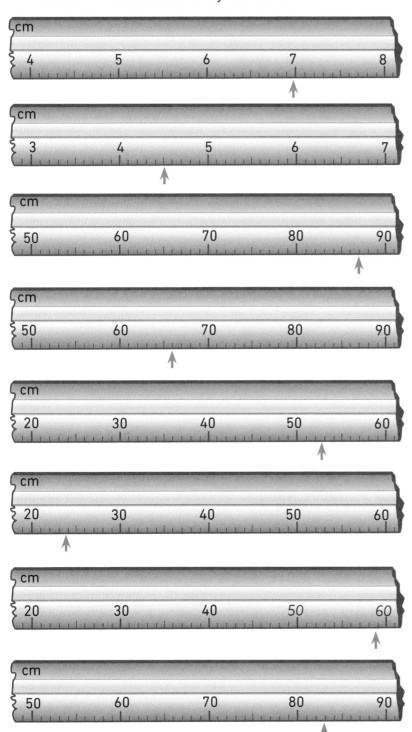

cm

4   5   6   7   8

cm

3   4   5   6   7

cm

50   60   70   80   90

cm

50   60   70   80   90

cm

20   30   40   50   60

cm

20   30   40   50   60

cm

20   30   40   50   60

cm

50   60   70   80   90

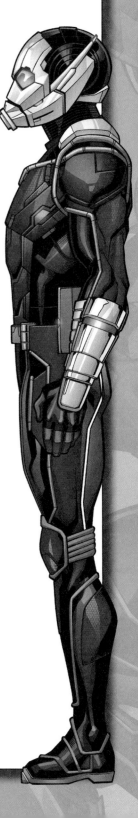

Parts of a set

Write the fraction. $\dfrac{3}{4}$ part of the set / whole set

How many ?   3

How many shields in all?   4

Circle the fraction that shows the shaded part of the set.

$\dfrac{1}{3}$ $\dfrac{2}{3}$ $\dfrac{3}{2}$ $\dfrac{3}{5}$ $\dfrac{4}{5}$ $\dfrac{1}{5}$

$\dfrac{1}{4}$ $\dfrac{3}{4}$ $\dfrac{1}{2}$ $\dfrac{4}{5}$ $\dfrac{1}{5}$ $\dfrac{3}{5}$

Write the fraction that shows the shaded part of the set.

$\dfrac{}{3}$ $\dfrac{}{5}$ $\dfrac{}{4}$

$\dfrac{}{5}$ $\dfrac{}{7}$

$\dfrac{}{8}$ $\dfrac{}{6}$  $\dfrac{}{8}$

Bar graphs and pictographs

Look at the bar graph and answer the question.

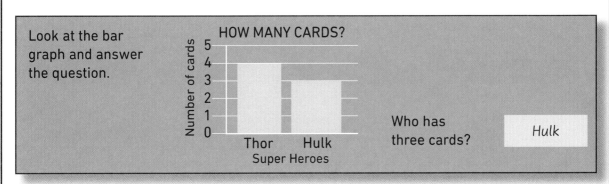

HOW MANY CARDS?

Number of cards

Thor | Hulk
Super Heroes

Who has three cards?

| Hulk |

Look at the bar graph and answer the questions.

CRIMINALS CAUGHT

Number of criminals

Hulk | Iron Man | Spidey | Thor | Ant-Man
Super Heroes

How many criminals did Iron Man catch?

Who caught eight criminals?

Who caught fewer criminals than Thor?

Who caught the most criminals?

How many criminals were caught in total?

Look at the pictograph and answer the questions.

   each badge stands for 2 children

CHILDREN'S FAVORITE SUPER HEROES

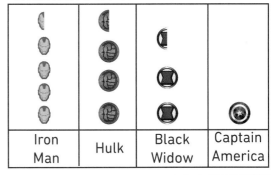

| Iron Man | Hulk | Black Widow | Captain America |

How many children like Captain America the most?

Which Super Hero is the favorite of 5 children?

How many more children like Iron Man than the Hulk?

Who is the most popular Super Hero?

Symmetry

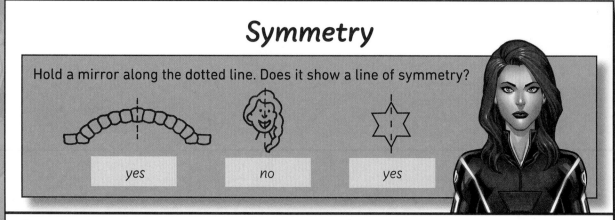
Does the dotted line show a line of symmetry? Write yes or no.

60

Symmetry

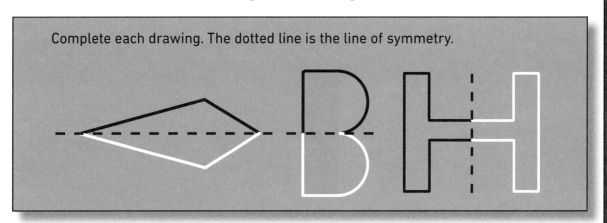

Complete each drawing. The dotted line is the line of symmetry.

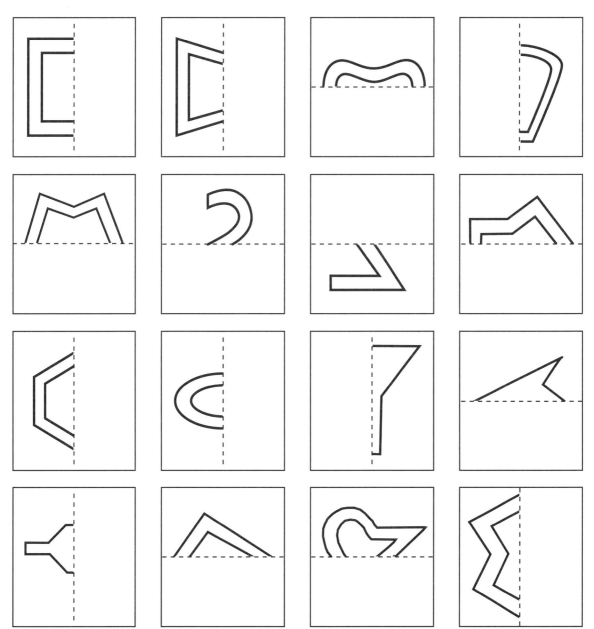

Doubles

Write the missing numbers.

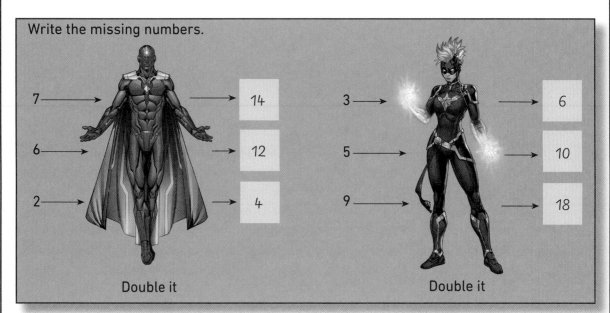

7 → 14

6 → 12

2 → 4

Double it

3 → 6

5 → 10

9 → 18

Double it

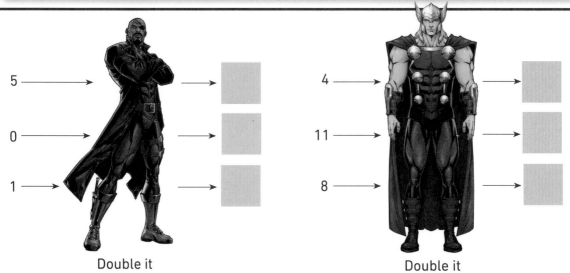

5 →

0 →

1 →

Double it

4 →

11 →

8 →

Double it

What has been doubled? Write the missing number.

Double 5 is 10   Double 2 4

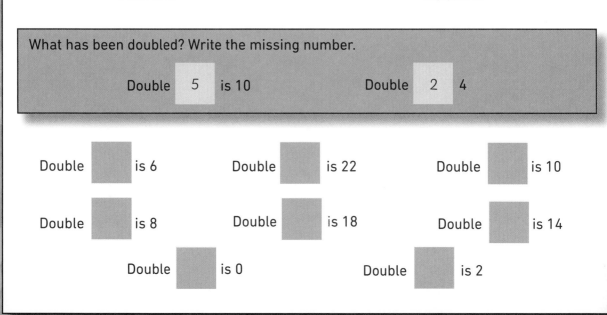

Double [ ] is 6   Double [ ] is 22   Double [ ] is 10

Double [ ] is 8   Double [ ] is 18   Double [ ] is 14

Double [ ] is 0   Double [ ] is 2

Addition grid

Draw rings around the pairs of numbers that add up to 20.

You can draw the rings up, down, side to side, or diagonal.

15	5	3	10	10	4	19
8	6	20	0	9	1	10
12	13	7	12	0	16	1
4	5	10	16	4	5	10
9	2	18	7	20	3	10
11	3	3	1	0	11	9
17	1	1	19	3	18	11

Answer Section with Parents' Notes

Grade 2
ages 7-8
Workbook

This section provides answers to all the activities in this book. These pages will enable you to mark your children's work, or they can be used by your children if they prefer to do their own marking.

The notes for each page helpexplain common errors and problems and, where appropriate, indicate the kind of practice needed toensure that your children understand where and how they have made errors.

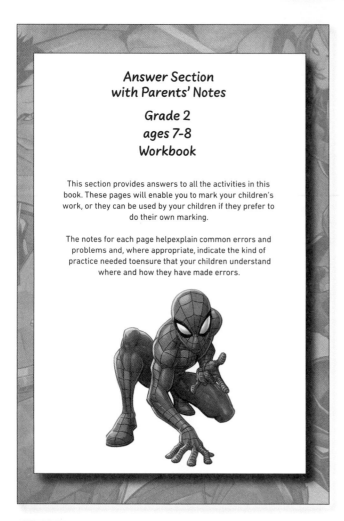

Counting by 1s, 10s, and 100s

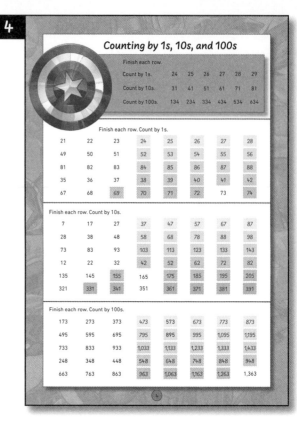

Finish each row.

Count by 1s.	24	25	26	27	28	29
Count by 10s.	31	41	51	61	71	81
Count by 100s.	134	234	334	434	534	634

Finish each row. Count by 1s.

21	22	23	24	25	26	27	28
49	50	51	52	53	54	55	56
81	82	83	84	85	86	87	88
35	36	37	38	39	40	41	42
67	68	69	70	71	72	73	74

Finish each row. Count by 10s.

7	17	27	37	47	57	67	87
28	38	48	58	68	78	88	98
73	83	93	103	113	123	133	143
12	22	32	42	52	62	72	82
135	145	155	165	175	185	195	205
321	331	341	351	361	371	381	391

Finish each row. Count by 100s.

173	273	373	473	573	673	773	873
495	595	695	795	895	995	1,095	1,195
733	833	933	1,033	1,133	1,233	1,333	1,433
248	348	448	548	648	748	848	948
663	763	863	963	1,063	1,163	1,263	1,363

For each row, children should realize that they need only increase the digit in the appropriate place value by 1. Some may have difficulty with a number such as 93 when they have to increase by ten, or a number such as 933 when they have to increase by 100.

Counting by 2s

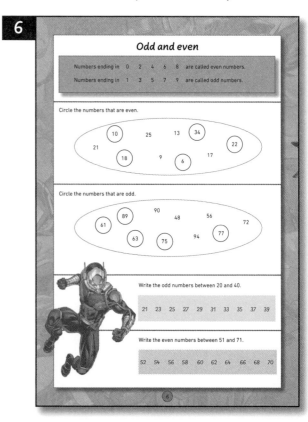

| Count by 2s. | 12 | 14 | 16 | 18 | 20 | 22 |
| Count by 2s. | 31 | 33 | 35 | 37 | 39 | 41 |

Finish each row. Count by 2s.

14	16	18	20	22	24	26	28
33	35	37	39	41	43	45	47
17	19	21	23	25	27	29	31
56	58	60	62	64	66	68	70
12	14	16	18	20	22	24	26
79	81	83	85	87	89	91	93

Finish each row. Count by 2s.

70	72	74	76	78	80	82	84
31	33	35	37	39	41	43	45
22	24	26	28	30	32	34	36
58	60	62	64	66	68	70	72
45	47	49	51	53	55	57	59
69	71	73	75	77	79	81	83

Finish each row. Count by 2s.

20	22	24	26	28	30	32	34
46	48	50	52	54	56	58	60
83	85	87	89	91	93	95	97
6	8	10	12	14	16	18	20
9	11	13	15	17	19	21	23
56	58	60	62	64	66	68	70

As on the previous page, some children will need help crossing a tens or hundreds "border." Show them counting by 2s by counting by 1 two times.

Odd and even

| Numbers ending in | 0 | 2 | 4 | 6 | 8 | are called even numbers. |
| Numbers ending in | 1 | 3 | 5 | 7 | 9 | are called odd numbers. |

Circle the numbers that are even.

(10) 25 13 (34) 21 (22) (18) 9 (6) 17

Circle the numbers that are odd.

90
(89) 48 56 72
(61) (63) (75) 94 (77)

Write the odd numbers between 20 and 40.

21 23 25 27 29 31 33 35 37 39

Write the even numbers between 51 and 71.

52 54 56 58 60 62 64 66 68 70

Children should realize that all even numbers are multiples of 2 and that they can all be divided by 2 to give a whole-number quotient. Odd numbers cannot be divided by two. If unsure, a child can use counters and try to share them equally.

Reading and writing numbers

Write this number in words. 278 *two hundred seventy-eight*
Write this number in digits. four hundred twelve 412

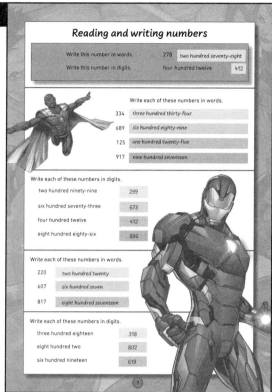

Write each of these numbers in words.

334 *three hundred thirty-four*
689 *six hundred eighty-nine*
125 *one hundred twenty-five*
917 *nine hundred seventeen*

Write each of these numbers in digits.

two hundred ninety-nine 299
six hundred seventy-three 673
four hundred twelve 412
eight hundred eighty-six 886

Write each of these numbers in words.

220 *two hundred twenty*
607 *six hundred seven*
817 *eight hundred seventeen*

Write each of these numbers in digits.

three hundred eighteen 318
eight hundred two 802
six hundred nineteen 619

Children may miss the significance of a 0 in the tens position, and write 607 as six hundred seventy, and eight hundred two may be written as 820. Have them read the numbers they have written and then write those numbers as words, or vice versa.

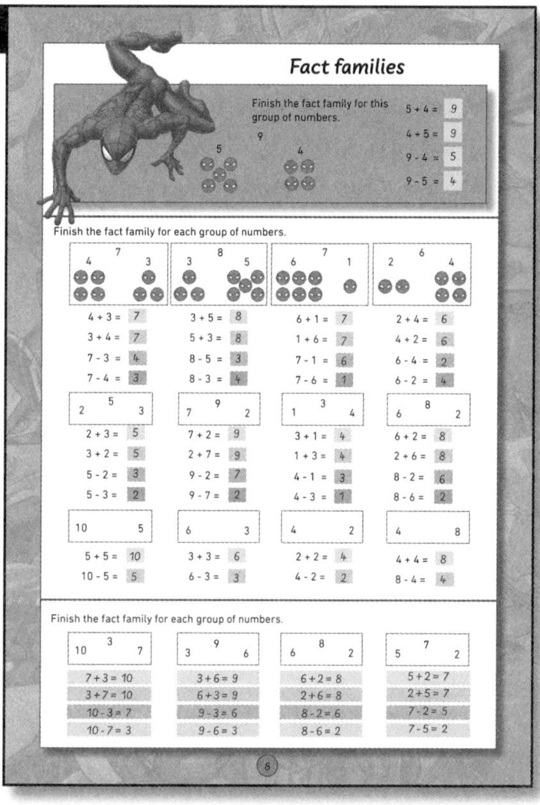

Fact families

Finish the fact family for this group of numbers. 9 5 4

5 + 4 = 9
4 + 5 = 9
9 − 4 = 5
9 − 5 = 4

Finish the fact family for each group of numbers.

7 4 3

4 + 3 = 7
3 + 4 = 7
7 − 3 = 4
7 − 4 = 3

8 3 5

3 + 5 = 8
5 + 3 = 8
8 − 5 = 3
8 − 3 = 5

7 6 1

6 + 1 = 7
1 + 6 = 7
7 − 1 = 6
7 − 6 = 1

6 2 4

2 + 4 = 6
4 + 2 = 6
6 − 4 = 2
6 − 2 = 4

5 2 3

2 + 3 = 5
3 + 2 = 5
5 − 2 = 3
5 − 3 = 2

9 7 2

7 + 2 = 9
2 + 7 = 9
9 − 2 = 7
9 − 7 = 2

3 1 4

3 + 1 = 4
1 + 3 = 4
4 − 1 = 3
4 − 3 = 1

8 6 2

6 + 2 = 8
2 + 6 = 8
8 − 2 = 6
8 − 6 = 2

10 5 5

5 + 5 = 10
10 − 5 = 5

6 3 3

3 + 3 = 6
6 − 3 = 3

4 2 2

2 + 2 = 4
4 − 2 = 2

4 4 8

4 + 4 = 8
8 − 4 = 4

Finish the fact family for each group of numbers.

10 3 7

7 + 3 = 10
3 + 7 = 10
10 − 3 = 7
10 − 7 = 3

9 3 6

3 + 6 = 9
6 + 3 = 9
9 − 3 = 6
9 − 6 = 3

8 6 2

6 + 2 = 8
2 + 6 = 8
8 − 2 = 6
8 − 6 = 2

7 5 2

5 + 2 = 7
2 + 5 = 7
7 − 2 = 5
7 − 5 = 2

Children should understand that subtraction "undoes" addition. You may want to use counters to demonstrate addition fact families.

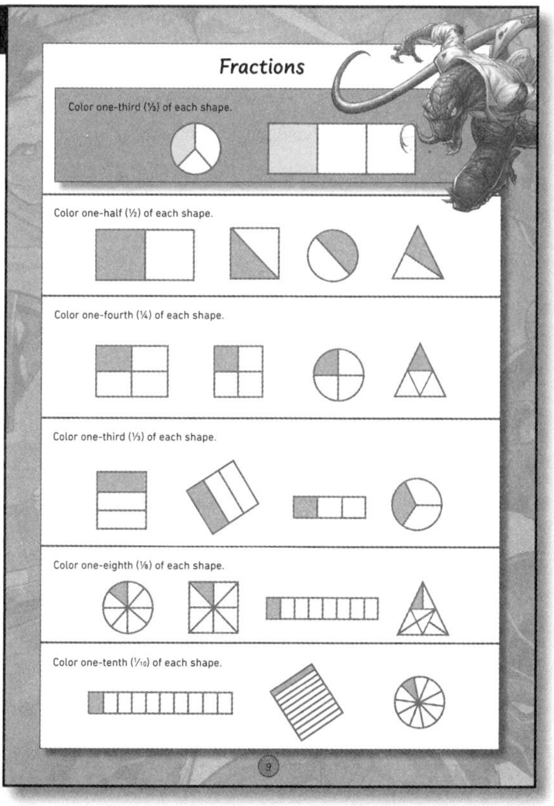

9

Fractions

Color one-third (⅓) of each shape.

Color one-half (½) of each shape.

Color one-fourth (¼) of each shape.

Color one-third (⅓) of each shape.

Color one-eighth (⅛) of each shape.

Color one-tenth (¹⁄₁₀) of each shape.

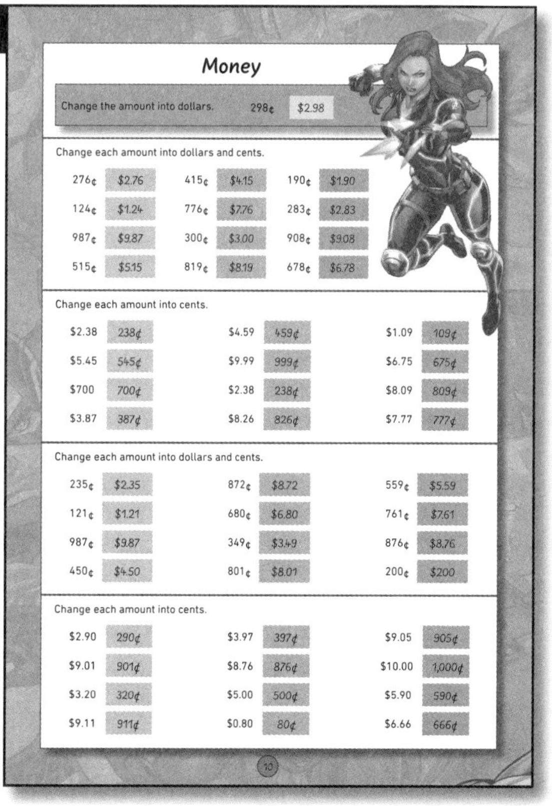

It does not matter if children color alternative sections than those shown above, as long as only one section in each shape is colored. Children should realize that the bottom number represents how many parts the whole has been divided into.

Money

Change the amount into dollars. 298¢ $2.98

Change each amount into dollars and cents.

276¢ $2.76   415¢ $4.15   190¢ $1.90
124¢ $1.24   776¢ $7.76   283¢ $2.83
987¢ $9.87   300¢ $3.00   908¢ $9.08
515¢ $5.15   819¢ $8.19   678¢ $6.78

Change each amount into cents.

$2.38 238¢ $4.59 459¢ $1.09 109¢
$5.45 545¢ $9.99 999¢ $6.75 675¢
$7.00 700¢ $2.38 238¢ $8.09 809¢
$3.87 387¢ $8.26 826¢ $7.77 777¢

Change each amount into dollars and cents.

235¢ $2.35   872¢ $8.72   559¢ $5.59
121¢ $1.21   680¢ $6.80   761¢ $7.61
987¢ $9.87   349¢ $3.49   876¢ $8.76
450¢ $4.50   801¢ $8.01   200¢ $2.00

Change each amount into cents.

$2.90 290¢ $3.97 397¢ $9.05 905¢
$9.01 901¢ $8.76 876¢ $10.00 1,000¢
$3.20 320¢ $5.00 500¢ $5.90 590¢
$9.11 911¢ $0.80 80¢ $6.66 666¢

Make sure that children understand that when they change cents into dollars and cents, they should include the dollar sign but not the cent sign: for example, $2.76.

Adding

Write the answer in the box.   35 + 20 = **55**

Write the answer in the box.

22 + 16 = **38**	12 + 28 = **40**	80 + 19 = **99**
49 + 23 = **72**	22 + 59 = **81**	23 + 42 = **65**
30 + 40 = **70**	69 + 13 = **82**	18 + 62 = **80**
36 + 61 = **97**	52 + 68 = **120**	12 + 39 = **51**

Write the answer in the box.

20 + 30 + 18 = **68**	40 + 20 + 17 = **77**
65 + 10 + 12 = **87**	77 + 10 + 7 = **94**
35 + 45 + 12 = **92**	70 + 20 + 12 = **102**
40 + 30 + 20 = **90**	49 + 18 + 17 = **84**
43 + 23 + 13 = **79**	28 + 27 + 26 = **81**
81 + 10 + 3 = **94**	50 + 28 + 12 = **90**

Write the answer in the box.

83¢ + 10¢ = **93¢**	63¢ + 34¢ = **97¢**	55¢ + 30¢ = **85¢**
70¢ + 17¢ = **87¢**	70¢ + 19¢ = **89¢**	60¢ + 19¢ = **79¢**
25¢ + 5¢ = **30¢**	18¢ + 17¢ = **35¢**	39¢ + 25¢ = **64¢**
49¢ + 18¢ = **67¢**	68¢ + 18¢ = **86¢**	54¢ + 12¢ = **66¢**

Write the answer in the box.

18 ft + 18 ft + 60 ft = **96 ft**	19 ft + 20 ft + 35 ft = **74 ft**
15 ft + 17 ft + 19 ft = **51 ft**	35 ft + 30 ft + 25 ft = **90 ft**

(11)

Children should be able to add quickly if they know that adding a 10s number requires adding only to the tens digit. Make sure that children include units (such as cents and feet) for problems in which units are given.

Adding

Write the answers between the lines.

27 + 8	12 + 6	69 + 9
35	**18**	**78**

Write the answers between the lines.

15 + 9	23 + 3	11 + 7	36 + 5
24	**26**	**18**	**41**
33 + 9	62 + 5	44 + 4	28 + 8
42	**67**	**48**	**36**
36 + 1	27 + 9	38 + 2	27 + 2
37	**36**	**40**	**29**

Write the answers between the lines.

12 + 12	28 + 27	23 + 33	18 + 33
24	**55**	**56**	**51**
43 + 43	38 + 27	24 + 66	45 + 23
86	**65**	**90**	**68**
63 + 13	15 + 29	73 + 10	14 + 19
76	**44**	**83**	**33**

(12)

Many of the problems require children to regroup. Children should make sure to add up the ones column first.

Subtracting

Write the answers in the boxes.   13 - 7 = **6**   23 - 21 = **2**

Write the answers in the boxes.

25 – 4 = **21**	34 – 6 = **28**	24 – 5 = **19**	15 – 8 = **7**
12 – 1 = **11**	21 – 15 = **6**	36 – 12 = **24**	34 – 6 = **28**
44 – 14 = **30**	24 – 17 = **7**	55 – 12 = **43**	18 – 0 = **18**
13 – 6 = **7**	45 – 7 = **38**	23 – 13 = **10**	12 – 7 = **5**
27 – 11 = **16**	13 – 11 = **2**	18 – 12 = **6**	33 – 12 = **21**

Write the answers in the boxes.

22¢ – 2¢ = **20¢**	18¢ – 7¢ = **11¢**	99¢ – 34¢ = **65¢**	23¢ – 16¢ = **7¢**
65¢ – 36¢ = **29¢**	22¢ – 11¢ = **11¢**	30¢ – 23¢ = **7¢**	88¢ – 17¢ = **71¢**
89¢ – 35¢ = **54¢**	56¢ – 46¢ = **10¢**	47¢ – 29¢ = **18¢**	46¢ – 13¢ = **33¢**
65¢ – 23¢ = **42¢**	63¢ – 9¢ = **54¢**	84¢ – 34¢ = **50¢**	55¢ – 42¢ = **13¢**
47¢ – 9¢ = **38¢**	19¢ – 11¢ = **8¢**	63¢ – 26¢ = **37¢**	72¢ – 12¢ = **60¢**

Write the answers in the boxes.

How much less than 34¢ is 11¢? **23¢**	How much less than 40 in. is 26 in.? **14 in.**
Take 16¢ away from 30¢. **14¢**	War Machine has 50¢. He spends 40¢ on candy. How much does he have left? **10¢**
How much is 60¢ minus 14¢? **46¢**	
Take away 28¢ from 44¢. **16¢**	What is the difference between 90 in. and 55 in.? **35 in.**
What is the difference between 70¢ and 25¢? **45¢**	

(13)

If children need to, they may rewrite each subtraction in vertical form.

14

Subtracting

Write the answers between the lines.

26 – 16	41 – 24	50 – 27
10	**17**	**23**

Write the answers between the lines.

37 – 24	51 – 35	70 – 47	63 – 48
13	**16**	**23**	**15**
42 – 24	55 – 36	43 – 30	60 – 37
18	**19**	**13**	**23**
57 – 38	35 – 16	73 – 54	46 – 38
19	**19**	**19**	**8**
38 – 26	53 – 45	60 – 36	58 – 47
12	**8**	**24**	**11**
63 – 45	47 – 38	80 – 57	55 – 48
18	**9**	**23**	**7**
50 – 18	70 – 36	51 – 24	64 – 46
32	**34**	**27**	**18**

(14)

In some of these exercises, children may incorrectly subtract the smaller digit from the larger one, when they should be subtracting the larger digit from the smaller one. In such cases, point out that they should regroup.

Estimating length

Circle the longest string.

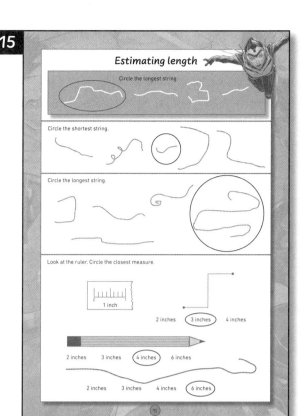

Circle the shortest string.

Circle the longest string.

Look at the ruler. Circle the closest measure.

1 inch

2 inches　(3 inches)　4 inches

2 inches　3 inches　(4 inches)　6 inches

2 inches　3 inches　4 inches　(6 inches)

15

Children should be able to compare the lengths by sight. For the last section of the page, allow them to use a benchmark (such as the length of one joint of a finger) to estimate length.

Addition properties

Circle the number that makes the sentence true.

___ + 3 = 3 　　　　25 + 41 = 41 + ___

(0)　3　6　　　　16　66　(25)

Circle the number that makes the sentence true.

___ + 3 = 6 　　　　15 + ___ = 20

0　(3)　6　　　　15　10　(5)

___ + 22 = 22 + 18 　　50 + 25 = 25 + ___

(18)　22　44　　　　25　(50)　75

___ + 19 = 19 　　　　80 + 40 = 40 + ___

19　(0)　1　　　　(80)　0　120

Complete the number sentences.

54 = 27 + 27 　　45 + 0 = 45 　　15 + 30 = 30 + 15

63 + 3 = 3 + 63 　　6 + 0 = 6 　　12 + 21 = 21 + 12

2 + 41 = 41 + 2 　　18 + 12 = 30 　　14 + 44 = 44 + 14

45 + 0 = 45 　　16 + 0 = 16 　　200 + 800 = 800 + 200

235 + 0 = 235 　　18 + 0 = 18 　　333 + 123 = 123 + 333

16

This page tests children's understanding of the zero property and the commutative property of addition. Make sure that children understand that the order of addends does not affect the answer.

Add or subtract?

Write + or - in the box.

8 - 7 = 1 　16 - 8 = 8 　6 + 7 = 13

Write + or - in the box.

4 + 4 = 8 　7 - 7 = 0 　8 - 6 = 2 　5 - 5 = 0

12 - 6 = 6 　10 - 4 = 6 　2 + 8 = 10 　22 - 7 = 15

8 + 6 = 14 　12 + 6 = 18 　3 + 6 = 9 　13 - 10 = 3

17 - 10 = 7 　14 - 4 = 10 　15 - 5 = 10 　8 + 10 = 18

Write the answer in the box.

I add 8 to a number and the answer is 9. What number did I start with? 　1

10 added to a number gives a total of 12. What is the number? 　2

I take 9 from a number and have 6 left. What number did I start with? 　15

14 added to a number makes 28. What is the number? 　14

I subtract 7 from a number and the answer is 14. What number did I start with? 　21

Two numbers add up to 19. One of the numbers is 8. What is the other number? 　11

Write + or - in the box.

15 - 8 = 7 　20 + 5 = 25 　30 - 30 = 0 　40 - 38 = 2

22 - 2 = 20 　24 - 2 = 22 　18 + 12 = 30 　66 - 16 = 50

35 + 6 = 41 　60 + 3 = 63 　30 + 26 = 56 　23 + 32 = 55

40 - 20 = 20 　34 - 2 = 32 　13 + 14 = 27 　34 - 5 = 29

17

Children must choose between addition and subtraction to solve each problem. If they make an error, have them substitute their answer in the problem to show them that the answer is not correct.

Subtracting

Write the answers between the lines.

739	685	788
− 221	− 202	− 345
518	483	443

Write the answers between the lines.

563	766	509	999
− 211	− 435	− 103	− 333
352	331	406	666

567	836	378	598
− 346	− 435	− 222	− 123
221	401	156	475

878	989	349	120
− 456	− 241	− 219	− 100
422	748	130	20

768	559	789	445
− 234	− 213	− 321	− 220
534	346	468	225

Write the answers between the lines.

$2.44	$8.76	$4.23	$5.51	$7.79
− $1.21	− $3.23	− $2.22	− $3.50	− $3.38
$1.23	$5.53	$2.01	$2.01	$4.41

18

Regrouping is not needed to subtract the numbers on this page. Discuss any mistakes with children to determine whether they are due to lapses of concentration or a basic misunderstanding of the concept.

19

Working with coins

Write the answers in the boxes.

Falcon has: one dime, one dime, one dime, one cent, one cent, one cent

Thor has: one dime, one dime, one dime, one dime, one dime

How much more does Thor have than Falcon?

$50¢ - 33¢ =$ | 17¢

Write the answers in the boxes.

Thor has these coins. quarter, quarter, one dime, five cents

How much more does Thor need to have $1? | 35¢

Falcon wants to buy a snack for half dollar. He has these coins. one cent, one dime, one cent, one cent, one dime, one dime

How much more does Falcon need? | 18¢

Peter Parker gives the shopkeeper $1.00 to buy a soda that cost 94¢. Peter Parker has two coins in his change. Which two coins does he have? | $1 | 5¢ nickel | 1¢ penny

Black Widow has three coins that add up to 36¢. Which three coins does she have? | 25¢ quarter | 10¢ dime | 1¢ penny

Iron Man is given these coins by a friend. quarter, quarter, one dime, five cents, one dime, five cents, quarter, one cent, one cent

How much more than one dollar does he have? | 7¢

Falcon has three coins that total 40¢. Which coins does Falcon have? | 25¢ quarter | 10¢ dime | 5¢ nickel

Iron Man has these coins. one dime, quarter, one dime

Thor has these coins. one dime, five cents, five cents

How much more does Iron Man have than Thor? | 25¢

Regrouping is not needed to subtract the numbers on this page. Discuss any mistakes with children to determine whether they are due to lapses of concentration or a basic misunderstanding of the concept of dollars.

20

Money problems

Look at these coins. one dime, one dime, one dime, one dime, One nickel

How much more is needed to make 75¢? | 30¢

How much is 15¢ and 19¢? | 34¢

Write the answers in the boxes.

What is the total of 40¢ and 50¢? | 90¢

What is 70¢ less 25¢? | 45¢

Hawkeye collects nickels and has 45¢ worth. How many nickels does he have? | 9 nickels

Doctor Strange has these coins. Which coin does he need to make $1.00? five cents, five cents, one dime, half dollar | 30¢ 3 dimes

Thor starts out with 90¢ but loses 35¢. How much does he have left? | 55¢

Captain America has four coins that add up to 17¢. Which coins does he have? | 10¢ dime | 5¢ nickel | 1¢ penny | 1¢ penny

Which four of these coins add up to $0.86? One nickel, one cent, one dime, quarter, half dollar | 50¢ half dollar | 25¢ quarter | 10¢ dime | 1¢ penny

How much is four groups of coins with 1 dime and 1 nickel in each group? | 60¢

These coins are shared equally by two mutants. How much does each mutant get? quarter, quarter, One nickel, One nickel | 30¢

Write the answers in the boxes.

25¢ + 25¢ = 50¢	20¢ + 26¢ = 46¢	25¢ + 7¢ = 32¢
30¢ - 20¢ = 10¢	48¢ - 8¢ = 40¢	54¢ - 14¢ = 40¢
15¢ + 55¢ = 70¢	72¢ + 13¢ = 85¢	78¢ - 28¢ = 50¢

If children have difficulty with these exercises, you may want to use actual coins to work with.

21

Measurement problems

yardstick, measuring wheel, tape measure, ruler

Which measuring tool would be best to measure a garden? | measuring wheel

Which measuring tool would be best for measuring each item?

Loki's sceptre | tape measure

Doctor Strange | yardstick

Vision's boot | tape measure

Ultron's arm | yardstick

Hawkeye's arrows | ruler

Round a building | measuring wheel

Thor's hammer | yardstick

The star on Captain America's shield | ruler

Thor's cloak | tape measure

Although it is possible to measure most of these items with any of the instruments the question is "which is best?". Help children understand why a tape measure is more useful than a ruler for measuring curved lengths.

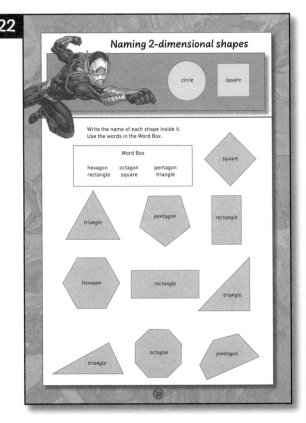

Naming 2-dimensional shapes

circle | square

Write the name of each shape inside it. Use the words in the Word Box.

Word Box

hexagon   octagon   pentagon
rectangle   square   triangle

square

triangle | pentagon | rectangle

hexagon | rectangle | triangle

triangle | octagon | pentagon

If children have difficulty identifying any of the shapes, have them count the number of sides of the shape first.

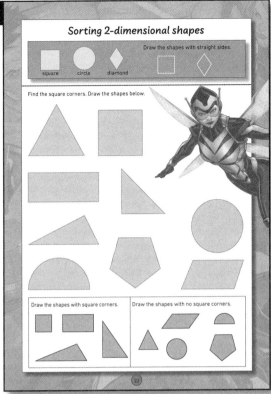

Sorting 2-dimensional shapes

| square | circle | diamond | Draw the shapes with straight sides. |

Find the square corners. Draw the shapes below.

Draw the shapes with square corners.

Draw the shapes with no square corners.

Children should find the right angles for most of the shapes without much difficulty. The orientation of some of the shapes may confuse children, for example, the pentagon. Explain that the shape remains the same regardless of orientation.

24

Picture graphs

Look at this picture graph. Then answer the questions.

JEAN GREY'S PENS

| Clear |
| Red |
| Blue |
| Yellow |
| Black |

How many blue pens does Jean Grey have? **4**

Does Jean have more blue pens or yellow pens? **blue**

How many pens does Jean have in all? **16**

Look at this picture graph. Then answer the questions.

BOOKS ON DOCTOR STRANGE'S SHELF

| Art |
| Comics |
| History |
| Science |
| Sports |

How many science books does the doctor have? **6**

Does he have more books about art than history? **no**

How many more science books does he have than books about sports? **3**

How many comic books and history books does Doctor Strange have? **5**

Look at this picture graph. Then answer the questions.

NUMBER OF TIMES CHARACTERS WERE SEEN IN TIMES SQUARE

| Captain America |
| Captain Marvel |
| Iron Man |
| Black Widow |

Which character was seen most times in Times Square? **Iron Man**

How many more times was Captain Marvel seen than Black Widow? **2 times**

How many more times was Iron Man seen than Captain America? **4 times**

How many times were the characters seen in all? **18**

Children need to count the items for each category, and then add, subtract, and compare data.

25

Equations

Circle the correct number sentence.

7 + 3 = 10   **4 + 3 = 7**   4 – 3 = 1   2 + 4 = 6   2 + 3 = 5   **5 – 3 = 2**

Circle the correct addition sentence.

5 + 2 = 7   **3 + 2 = 5**   3 – 2 = 1   4 + 2 = 6   5 – 1 = 4   **5 + 1 = 6**

Circle the correct subtraction sentence.

3 + 3 = 6   3 – 3 = 0   **6 – 3 = 3**   **6 – 2 = 4**   6 + 2 = 8   4 – 2 = 2

Circle the correct number sentence.

9 – 3 = 6   5 – 3 = 2   6 – 3 = 3   5 – 2 = 3   **2 + 5 = 7**   7 – 5 = 2

6 – 4 = 2   **4 + 2 = 6**   6 + 2 = 8   5 – 1 = 4   4 + 5 = 9   **9 – 4 = 5**

For the final section, make sure that children understand that characters approaching each other represent addition and characters moving away from each other represent subtraction.

26

Location on grid

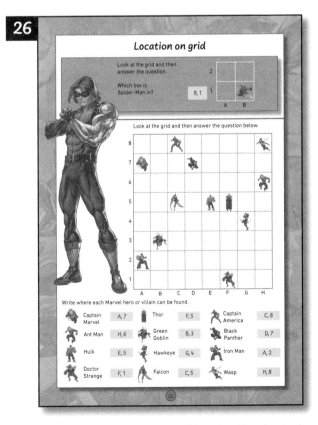

Look at the grid and then answer the question.

Which box is Spider-Man in? **B, 1**

Look at the grid and then answer the question below.

Write where each Marvel hero or villain can be found.

Captain Marvel	A, 7	Thor	F, 5	Captain America	C, 8
Ant Man	H, 6	Green Goblin	B, 3	Black Panther	D, 7
Hulk	E, 5	Hawkeye	G, 4	Iron Man	A, 2
Doctor Strange	F, 1	Falcon	C, 5	Wasp	H, 8

To label the squares on the grid, children should understand that the letter should precede the number. This will prepare them to learn about coordinates on graphs, where the value from the x-axis is written before the value from the y-axis.

27

Placing on grid

Draw a ✳ in B, 2

Look at the grid and then answer the question below.

Draw each picture in the correct box on the grid.

- △ in B, 4
- ○ in H, 7
- ▲ in D, 5
- ⛰ in A, 6
- □ in C, 3
- ⬭ in E, 8
- ■ in F, 2
- ◉ in G, 1
- ◎ in B, 7
- ⌣ in H, 4
- ● in D, 8
- ⌣ in A, 2

Children should be careful to draw the pictures within the boxes, not on the lines.

28

Counting by 3s, 4s, and 5s

Find the pattern. Continue each row.

Count by 3s.	12	15	18	21	24	27	30
Count by 4s.	36	32	28	24	20	16	12
Count by 5s.	35	40	45	50	55	60	65

Find the pattern. Continue each row.

9	12	15	18	21	24	27	30
0	4	8	12	16	20	24	28
25	30	35	40	45	50	55	60
71	74	77	80	83	86	89	92
76	72	68	64	60	56	52	48
70	75	80	85	90	95	100	105
14	17	20	23	26	29	32	35
21	18	15	12	9	6	3	0
35	30	25	20	15	10	5	0
84	80	76	72	68	64	60	56
22	27	32	37	42	47	52	57
29	33	37	41	45	49	53	57
44	39	34	29	24	19	14	9
77	80	83	86	89	92	95	98
100	95	90	85	80	75	70	

Some of the patterns show an increase, while others show a decrease. Children should be able to complete these questions using mental math.

29

Adding

Write the answer between the lines.

200	320	325
+ 200	+ 226	+ 324
400	546	649

Write the answer between the lines.

700	400	200	200	600
+ 200	+ 400	+ 400	+ 300	+ 100
900	800	600	500	700

440	320	660	460	260
+ 220	+ 430	+ 330	+ 220	+ 230
660	750	990	680	490

376	566	464	701	324
+ 223	+ 333	+ 234	+ 108	+ 601
599	899	698	809	925

484	221	407	417	105
+ 101	+ 261	+ 370	+ 280	+ 802
585	482	777	697	907

$4.42	$3.07	$4.40	$3.09	$3.20
+ $0.22	+ $2.21	+ $2.35	+ $2.50	+ $3.25
$4.64	$5.28	$6.75	$5.59	$6.45

None of these addition problems require regrouping.

30

Comparing and ordering

Write these numbers in order, starting with the smallest.

| 431 | 678 | 273 | 586 | 273 | 431 | 586 | 678 |

Write these numbers in order, starting with the smallest.

876	245	374	740	245	374	740	876
748	387	123	267	123	267	387	748
349	338	298	309	298	309	338	349
387	972	836	487	387	487	836	972
879	341	342	897	341	342	879	897
298	973	242	556	242	298	556	973
874	478	847	748	478	748	847	874
237	327	273	372	237	273	327	372
209	204	323	342	204	209	323	342
342	243	434	234	234	243	342	434
24	23	42	98	23	24	42	98
502	52	250	520	52	250	502	520
657	576	764	234	234	576	657	764
309	903	93	39	39	93	309	903
667	676	766	666	666	667	676	766

Make sure that children do not simply order the numbers according to the first digits.

31

Comparing and ordering

Circle the numbers that are greater than 200.

(232) 99 (201) 211 199

Circle the numbers that are greater than 710.

(711) (799) 777 709 700

Circle the numbers that are less than 550.

600 (500) (507) 528 550

Circle the numbers that are between 490 and 510.

511 480 520 (505) (499)

Circle the amounts that are greater than $1.00.

($1.08) 99¢ $0.85 105¢ ($1.99)

Circle the amounts that are less than $2.50.

251¢ ($2.48) ($1.99) $2.55 (245¢)

Circle the amounts that are between $1.85 and $2.00.

(186¢) 167¢ $3.00 $1.83 (195¢)

Children should make sure to circle all the numbers or amounts that satisfy each question. For the final question, children may want to rename $1.85 and $2.00 as cents.

32

Missing addends

Write the missing addend.

$6 + \boxed{7} = 13$

Write the missing addend.

$2 + 6 = 8$ $5 + 6 = 11$

$8 + \boxed{2} = 10$ $8 + 6 = 14$

Write the missing addend.

$4 + \boxed{4} = 8$	$6 + \boxed{9} = 15$	$6 + \boxed{3} = 9$	$5 + \boxed{6} = 11$
$2 + \boxed{5} = 7$	$2 + \boxed{8} = 10$	$5 + \boxed{7} = 12$	$3 + \boxed{5} = 8$
$7 + \boxed{7} = 14$	$3 + \boxed{6} = 9$	$3 + \boxed{3} = 6$	$8 + \boxed{4} = 12$
$8 + \boxed{3} = 11$	$3 + \boxed{7} = 10$	$6 + \boxed{5} = 11$	$1 + \boxed{1} = 2$
$6 + \boxed{6} = 12$	$5 + \boxed{1} = 6$	$3 + \boxed{1} = 4$	$8 + \boxed{4} = 12$
$8 + \boxed{8} = 16$	$8 + \boxed{9} = 17$	$2 + \boxed{3} = 5$	$3 + \boxed{4} = 7$
$4 + \boxed{2} = 6$	$4 + \boxed{9} = 13$	$5 + \boxed{8} = 13$	$7 + \boxed{9} = 16$
$6 + \boxed{7} = 13$	$8 + \boxed{6} = 14$	$5 + \boxed{9} = 14$	$7 + \boxed{8} = 15$
$9 + \boxed{9} = 18$	$7 + \boxed{8} = 15$	$4 + \boxed{6} = 10$	$2 + \boxed{1} = 3$

Children can use any method they wish to answer these problems—using related subtraction facts, counting, or number sense. They should be able to complete the page using mental math.

33

Reading tables

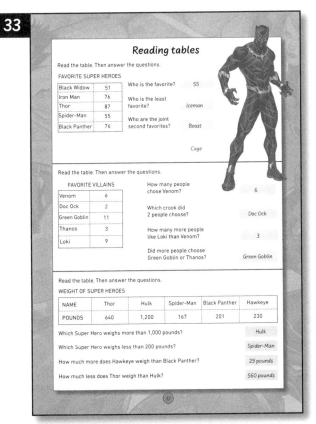

Read the table. Then answer the questions.

FAVORITE SUPER HEROES

Black Widow	51
Iron Man	76
Thor	87
Spider-Man	55
Black Panther	76

Who is the favorite? 55

Who is the least favorite? Iceman

Who are the joint second favorites? Beast

Cage

Read the table. Then answer the questions.

FAVORITE VILLAINS

Venom	6
Doc Ock	2
Green Goblin	11
Thanos	3
Loki	9

How many people chose Venom? 6

Which crook did 2 people choose? Doc Ock

How many more people like Loki than Venom? 3

Did more people choose Green Goblin or Thanos? Green Goblin

Read the table. Then answer the questions.

WEIGHT OF SUPER HEROES

NAME	Thor	Hulk	Spider-Man	Black Panther	Hawkeye
POUNDS	640	1,200	167	201	230

Which Super Hero weighs more than 1,000 pounds? Hulk

Which Super Hero weighs less than 200 pounds? Spider-Man

How much more does Hawkeye weigh than Black Panther? 29 pounds

How much less does Thor weigh than Hulk? 560 pounds

If children have difficulty reading the information in the last table, help them with one question, reading across the appropriate row and down the appropriate column, showing them the intersection of the two.

34

Extending geometric patterns

Circle the next three squares in each pattern.

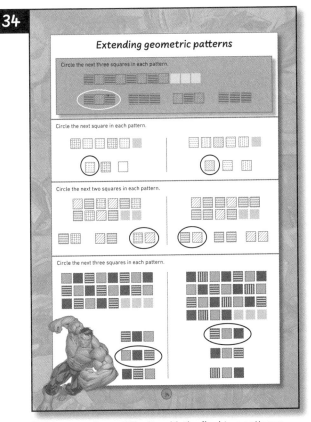

Circle the next square in each pattern.

Circle the next two squares in each pattern.

Circle the next three squares in each pattern.

Children may have difficulty with the final two patterns. Point out that the patterns run horizontally and diagonally.

35

Adding

Write the answer in each box.

22 + 18 + 11 = 51   18 + 12 + 20 = 50

Write the answer in each box.

22 + 35 + 20 = 77	60 + 15 + 15 = 90	16 + 10 + 30 = 56
42 + 20 + 10 = 72	15 + 15 + 15 = 45	13 + 12 + 15 = 40
33 + 22 + 23 = 78	13 + 19 + 20 = 52	13 + 14 + 15 = 42
22 + 20 + 40 = 82	23 + 10 + 7 = 40	15 + 15 + 60 = 90
12 + 13 + 18 = 43	10 + 15 + 9 = 34	12 + 34 + 44 = 90
15 + 21 + 32 = 68	35 + 35 + 7 = 77	20 + 24 + 15 = 59
31 + 22 + 16 = 69	22 + 23 + 14 = 59	35 + 45 + 9 = 89
52 + 18 + 12 = 82	15 + 21 + 22 = 58	21 + 21 + 16 = 58
40 + 30 + 10 = 80	30 + 40 + 20 = 90	10 + 20 + 60 = 90
28 + 11 + 60 = 99	15 + 46 + 23 = 94	23 + 34 + 16 = 73
22 + 23 + 24 = 69	13 + 70 + 11 = 94	11 + 14 + 50 = 75
14 + 24 + 34 = 72	24 + 25 + 50 = 99	31 + 38 + 20 = 89

Write the answer in each box.

5 + 6 + 7 + 8 = 26	2 + 2 + 5 + 7 = 16
3 + 5 + 7 + 9 = 24	5 + 8 + 9 + 2 = 24
2 + 4 + 6 + 8 = 20	8 + 7 + 8 + 9 = 32
3 + 6 + 6 + 3 = 18	4 + 9 + 9 + 8 = 30

For these questions, some children may want to find partial sums first.

Adding

Write the answer in the box.

34 + 13	26 + 15	73 + 27
47	41	100

Write the answer in the box. Regroup if needed.

22 + 13 = 35	43 + 23 = 66	53 + 26 = 79	52 + 16 = 68
37 + 20 = 57	72 + 23 = 95	32 + 28 = 60	45 + 24 = 69
50 + 28 = 78	31 + 9 = 40	28 + 17 = 45	50 + 45 = 95
56 + 16 = 72	28 + 38 = 66	61 + 16 = 77	51 + 13 = 64
39 + 39 = 78	74 + 12 = 86	53 + 28 = 81	43 + 12 = 55
28 + 13 = 41	44 + 28 = 72	29 + 16 = 45	56 + 17 = 73
23 + 29 = 52	33 + 12 = 45	23 + 57 = 80	55 + 15 = 70
29 + 24 = 53	37 + 27 = 64	85 + 14 = 99	28 + 23 = 51
46 + 54 = 100	38 + 50 = 88	27 + 37 = 64	26 + 19 = 45

Many of the problems require regrouping. Make sure that children do not neglect to add 10 to the tens columns when they regroup.

37

Subtracting

Write the answer in the box.

54 − 12 = 42   51 − 21 = 30

Write the answer in the box.

33 − 16 = 17	46 − 12 = 34	55 − 31 = 24	58 − 32 = 26
76 − 31 = 45	48 − 23 = 25	66 − 21 = 45	73 − 25 = 48
62 − 33 = 29	71 − 28 = 43	45 − 35 = 10	79 − 33 = 46
48 − 25 = 23	66 − 16 = 50	36 − 13 = 23	99 − 90 = 9
67 − 27 = 40	55 − 36 = 19	68 − 23 = 45	59 − 51 = 8

Write the answer in the box.

34¢ − 24¢ = 10¢	46¢ − 21¢ = 25¢	55¢ − 44¢ = 11¢	67¢ − 43¢ = 24¢
24¢ − 18¢ = 6¢	74¢ − 31¢ = 43¢	88¢ − 34¢ = 54¢	99¢ − 22¢ = 77¢
33¢ − 23¢ = 10¢	66¢ − 24¢ = 42¢	77¢ − 41¢ = 36¢	35¢ − 31¢ = 4¢
64¢ − 25¢ = 39¢	48¢ − 33¢ = 15¢	56¢ − 34¢ = 22¢	44¢ − 27¢ = 17¢
45¢ − 23¢ = 22¢	74¢ − 24¢ = 50¢	57¢ − 16¢ = 41¢	12¢ − 4¢ = 8¢

Write the answer in the box.

How much is 90¢ minus 35¢? 55¢

Take 56¢ away from $1.00. 44¢

How much is 95¢ minus 44¢? 51¢

Take away 87¢ from 99¢. 12¢

What is the difference between 56¢ and $1.21? 65¢

How much less than 98 in. is 22 in.? 76 in.   Take away 58 in. from 90 in. 32 in.

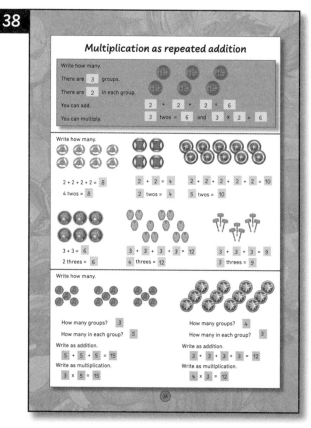

The Black Widow has 45¢. She spends 30¢ on candy. How much does she have left? 15¢

For the money problems, make sure that children include units in their answers.

Multiplication as repeated addition

Write how many.

There are 3 groups.

There are 2 in each group.

You can add.   2 + 2 + 2 = 6

You can multiply.   3 twos = 6 and 3 × 2 = 6

Write how many.

2 + 2 + 2 + 2 = 8
4 twos = 8

2 + 2 = 4
2 twos = 4

2 + 2 + 2 + 2 + 2 = 10
5 twos = 10

3 + 3 = 6
2 threes = 6

3 + 3 + 3 + 3 = 12
4 threes = 12

3 + 3 + 3 = 9
3 threes = 9

Write how many.

How many groups? 3
How many in each group? 5
Write as addition.
5 + 5 + 5 = 15
Write as multiplication.
3 × 5 = 15

How many groups? 4
How many in each group? 3
Write as addition.
3 + 3 + 3 + 3 = 12
Write as multiplication.
4 × 3 = 12

This page reinforces the 2 and 3 times tables. Children can count the items shown to verify their addition.

39

Choose the operation

Put either + or - in the box to make each answer correct.

13 **+** 13 = 26   24 **−** 14 = 10   28 **+** 12 = 40

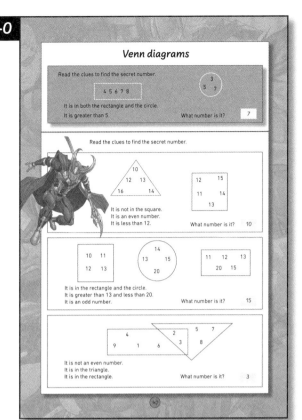

Put either + or - in the box to make each answer correct.

30 **+** 19 = 49	21 **−** 8 = 13	18 **−** 11 = 7	29 **+** 23 = 52
40 **−** 25 = 15	34 **+** 16 = 50	65 **−** 25 = 40	22 **+** 32 = 54
19 **+** 17 = 36	45 **−** 13 = 32	48 **−** 12 = 36	47 **+** 12 = 59
45 **−** 20 = 25	79 **−** 22 = 57	84 **−** 32 = 52	16 **+** 16 = 32
45 **−** 45 = 0	45 **+** 45 = 90	39 **+** 54 = 93	73 **−** 34 = 39

Write the answer in the box.

I add 13 to a number and the answer is 50. What number did I start with? **37**

67 added to a number makes 80. What is the number? **13**

45 added to a number gives a total of 64. What is the number? **19**

I subtract 35 from a number and the result is 24. What number did I start with? **59**

I take 22 away from a number and have 15 left. What number did I start with? **37**

Two numbers add up to 55. One of the numbers is 11. What is the other number? **44**

Two numbers are added together and the total is 45. One of the numbers is 22. What is the other number? **23**

After spending 45¢, I have 50¢ left. How much did I start with? **95¢**

Write + or - in the box.

17¢ **+** 25¢ = 42¢	34¢ **−** 17¢ = 19¢	82¢ **−** 41¢ = 41¢
65¢ **−** 65¢ = 0¢	25¢ **−** 13¢ = 12¢	60¢ **−** 46¢ = 14¢
54¢ **+** 18¢ = 72¢	28¢ **+** 24¢ = 52¢	54¢ **−** 7¢ = 37¢
43¢ **+** 23¢ = 66¢	63¢ **−** 37¢ = 26¢	45¢ **+** 23¢ = 68¢

Children should realize that if the answer is larger than the first number then they must add, and if the answer if smaller than the first number then they must subtract. They should check some of their answers to make sure that they are correct.

40

Venn diagrams

Read the clues to find the secret number.

4 5 6 7 8   (circle: 3 5 7)

It is in both the rectangle and the circle.
It is greater than 5.   What number is it? **7**

Read the clues to find the secret number.

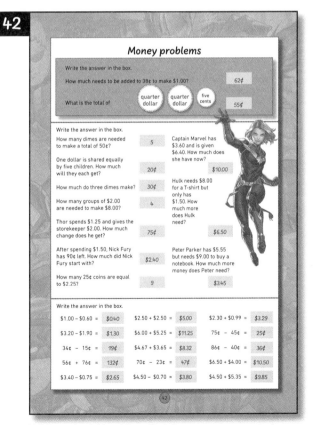

Triangle: 10, 12 13, 16 14 — Square: 12 15, 11 14, 13

It is not in the square.
It is an even number.
It is less than 12.   What number is it? **10**

Rectangle: 10 11, 12 13 — Circle: 14, 13 15, 20 — Rectangle: 11 12 13, 20 15

It is in the rectangle and the circle.
It is greater than 13 and less than 20.
It is an odd number.   What number is it? **15**

Triangle/Rectangle: 4, 9 1 6, 2 3 8, 5 7

It is not an even number.
It is in the triangle.
It is in the rectangle.   What number is it? **3**

If children have difficulty, "walk" them through the example. The final question is a Venn diagram showing which numbers are in both figures. You may want to ask children which numbers are in both the triangle and the rectangle.

41

Working with coins

Black Widow has these coins: (five cents) (quarter) (half dollar)
How much more does she need to have $1.00? **20¢**

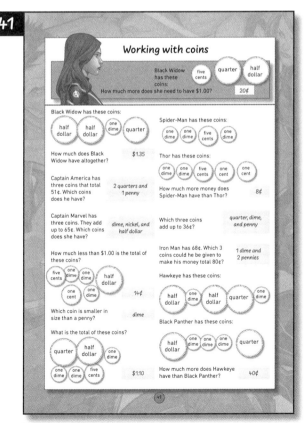

Black Widow has these coins: (half dollar) (half dollar) (one dime) (quarter)

How much does Black Widow have altogether? **$1.35**

Captain America has three coins that total 51¢. Which coins does he have? **2 quarters and 1 penny**

Captain Marvel has three coins. They add up to 65¢. Which coins does she have? **dime, nickel, and half dollar**

How much less than $1.00 is the total of these coins? (five cents) (one dime) (one dime) (half dollar) (one cent) (one dime) **14¢**

Which coin is smaller in size than a penny? **dime**

What is the total of these coins? (quarter) (half dollar) (one dime) (one dime) (one dime) (five cents) **$1.10**

Spider-Man has these coins: (one dime) (one dime) (five cents) (one dime)

Thor has these coins: (one dime) (one dime) (five cents) (one cent) (one cent)

How much more money does Spider-Man have than Thor? **8¢**

Which three coins add up to 36¢? **quarter, dime, and penny**

Iron Man has 68¢. Which 3 coins could he be given to make his money total 80¢? **1 dime and 2 pennies**

Hawkeye has these coins: (half dollar) (one dime) (half dollar) (quarter) (one dime)

Black Panther has these coins: (half dollar) (one dime) (one dime) (one dime) (quarter)

How much more does Hawkeye have than Black Panther? **40¢**

For some of these questions, children may have to use guess-and-check.

42

Money problems

Write the answer in the box.

How much needs to be added to 38¢ to make $1.00? **62¢**

What is the total of (quarter dollar) (quarter dollar) (five cents) **55¢**

Write the answer in the box.

How many dimes are needed to make a total of 50¢? **5**

One dollar is shared equally by five children. How much will they each get? **20¢**

How much do three dimes make? **30¢**

How many groups of $2.00 are needed to make $8.00? **4**

Thor spends $1.25 and gives the storekeeper $2.00. How much change does he get? **75¢**

After spending $1.50, Nick Fury has 90¢ left. How much did Nick Fury start with? **$2.40**

How many 25¢ coins are equal to $2.25? **9**

Captain Marvel has $3.60 and is given $6.40. How much does she have now? **$10.00**

Hulk needs $8.00 for a T-shirt but only has $1.50. How much more does Hulk need? **$6.50**

Peter Parker has $5.55 but needs $9.00 to buy a notebook. How much more money does Peter need? **$3.45**

Write the answer in the box.

$1.00 − $0.60 = **$0.40**	$2.50 + $2.50 = **$5.00**	$2.30 + $0.99 = **$3.29**
$3.20 − $1.90 = **$1.30**	$6.00 + $5.25 = **$11.25**	75¢ − 45¢ = **25¢**
34¢ − 15¢ = **19¢**	$4.67 + $3.65 = **$8.32**	86¢ − 40¢ = **36¢**
56¢ + 76¢ = **132¢**	70¢ − 23¢ = **47¢**	$6.50 + $4.00 = **$10.50**
$3.40 − $0.75 = **$2.65**	$4.50 − $0.70 = **$3.80**	$4.50 + $5.35 = **$9.85**

Children should be able to find the answers to most of these questions using mental math. In some cases, they may want to write the information as a subtraction problem.

Measurement problems

Write the answer in the box.

How many grams are equal to 1 kilogram? **1,000 g**

How many milliliters are the same as 1 liter? **1,000 ml**

Write the answer in the box. Use the information above.

How many grams are equal to 4 kilograms? **4000 g**

How many grams are the same as 0.7 kilograms? **700 g**

How many milliliters are the same as 3 liters? **3000 ml**

How many 250 ml glasses are equal to one liter? **4**

Is 800 ml more or less than half a liter? **more**

How many milliliters are the same as 0.5 liters? **500 ml**

How many 100 g weights are equal to 1 kilogram? **10**

How many grams are the same as 2.5 kg? **2500 g**

Is 400 ml more or less than half a liter? **less**

How many 300 ml jars are equal to 1.2 liters? **4**

Which unit of measurement would you use for each of these?
Choose from meter, milligram, milliliter, liter, kilometer, and kilogram.

To measure the mass of Hulk. **kilogram**

To measure the capacity of a bathtub. **liter**

To measure the capacity of a spoon. **milliliter**

To measure the mass of a spider. **milligram**

To measure the distance from Chicago to Detroit. **kilometer**

To measure the length of an airplane. **meter**

For most of these problems, children will have to count, rather than using multiplication or division. You may want to provide counters that children can use to represent the amounts.

2-dimensional shapes

Draw a circle. *Circle*

Draw a triangle. *Triangle*

Draw each shape in the box.

Rectangle | Circle | Square

Pentagon | Hexagon | Octagon

Triangle with three equal sides | Triangle with two equal sides | Triangle with no equal sides

Check the figures drawn by children for shape and appropriate length of sides.

Properties of polygons

Circle the polygon that has the same number of sides as the rectangle.

Circle the polygon that has the same number of sides as the first shape.

Circle the polygon that has a different number of sides.

Make sure that children understand that they are not looking for identical shapes, but figures with the given number of sides.

Pictographs

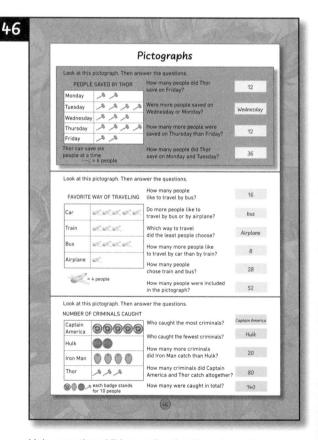

Look at this pictograph. Then answer the questions.

PEOPLE SAVED BY THOR

Monday	
Tuesday	
Wednesday	
Thursday	
Friday	

Thor can save six people at a time = 6 people

How many people did Thor save on Friday? **12**

Were more people saved on Wednesday or Monday? **Wednesday**

How many more people were saved on Thursday than Friday? **12**

How many people did Thor save on Monday and Tuesday? **36**

Look at this pictograph. Then answer the questions.

FAVORITE WAY OF TRAVELING

Car	
Train	
Bus	
Airplane	

= 4 people

How many people like to travel by bus? **16**

Do more people like to travel by bus or by airplane? **bus**

Which way to travel did the least people choose? **Airplane**

How many more people like to travel by car than by train? **8**

How many people chose train and bus? **28**

How many people were included in the pictograph? **52**

Look at this pictograph. Then answer the questions.

NUMBER OF CRIMINALS CAUGHT

Captain America	
Hulk	
Iron Man	
Thor	

each badge stands for 10 people

Who caught the most criminals? **Captain America**

Who caught the fewest criminals? **Hulk**

How many more criminals did Iron Man catch than Hulk? **20**

How many criminals did Captain America and Thor catch altogether? **80**

How many were caught in total? **140**

Make sure that children notice that the units on the scale are not in ones. To answer some of the questions, children will need to add, subtract, and compare data.

Most likely/least likely

Look at the pictures. Then answer the questions.

Which badge would you be least likely to pick without looking?

Which badge would you be most likely to pick without looking?

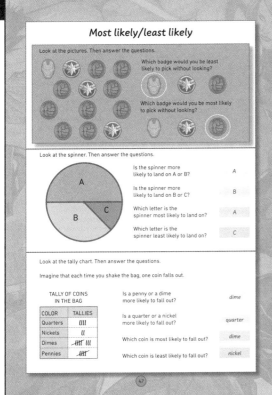

Look at the spinner. Then answer the questions.

Is the spinner more likely to land on A or B? — A

Is the spinner more likely to land on B or C? — B

Which letter is the spinner most likely to land on? — A

Which letter is the spinner least likely to land on? — C

Look at the tally chart. Then answer the questions.

Imagine that each time you shake the bag, one coin falls out.

TALLY OF COINS IN THE BAG			
COLOR	TALLIES		
Quarters	llll	Is a penny or a dime more likely to fall out?	dime
Nickels	ll	Is a quarter or a nickel more likely to fall out?	quarter
Dimes	llll lll	Which coin is most likely to fall out?	dime
Pennies	llll	Which coin is least likely to fall out?	nickel

Children should realize that the more of a particular item there is in a set, the more likely it is to be picked.

Square corners

Circle the square corners on all these shapes.

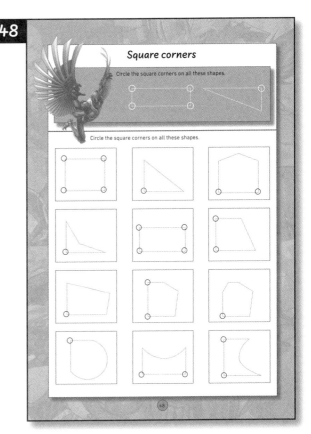

Circle the square corners on all these shapes.

Most of the right angles should be quite clear, but make sure that the children spot all of them, especially on the later figures.

Square corners

Circle the square corners on all these shapes.

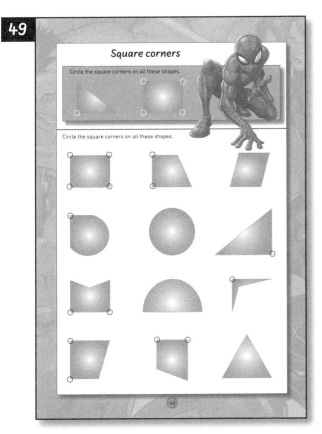

Circle the square corners on all these shapes.

See the comments for the previous page.

Place value

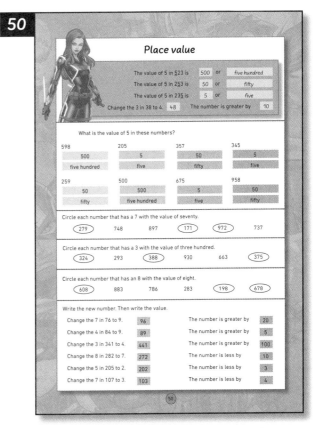

The value of 5 in 523 is — 500 — or — five hundred
The value of 5 in 253 is — 50 — or — fifty
The value of 5 in 235 is — 5 — or — five
Change the 3 in 38 to 4. — 48 — The number is greater by — 10

What is the value of 5 in these numbers?

598 — 500 — five hundred
205 — 5 — five
357 — 50 — fifty
345 — 5 — five
259 — 50 — fifty
500 — 500 — five hundred
675 — 5 — five
958 — 50 — fifty

Circle each number that has a 7 with the value of seventy.

(279) 748 897 (171) (972) 737

Circle each number that has a 3 with the value of three hundred.

(324) 293 (388) 930 663 (375)

Circle each number that has an 8 with the value of eight.

(608) 883 786 283 (198) (678)

Write the new number. Then write the value.

Change the 7 in 76 to 9.	96	The number is greater by	20
Change the 4 in 84 to 9.	89	The number is greater by	5
Change the 3 in 341 to 4.	441	The number is greater by	100
Change the 8 in 282 to 7.	272	The number is less by	10
Change the 5 in 205 to 2.	202	The number is less by	3
Change the 7 in 107 to 3.	103	The number is less by	4

If children make errors, have them read each number aloud before answering the question.

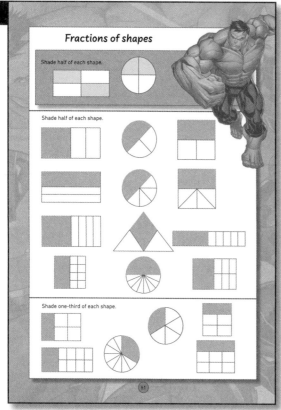

51

Fractions of shapes

Shade half of each shape.

Shade half of each shape.

Shade one-third of each shape.

Children may shade in any combination of the sections as long as the shaded area represents the fraction.

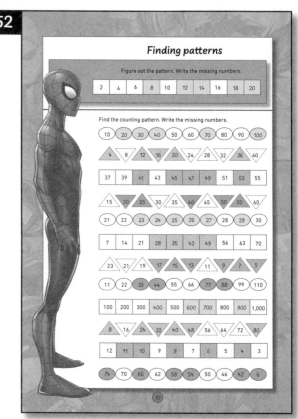

52

Finding patterns

Figure out the pattern. Write the missing numbers.

| 2 | 4 | 6 | 8 | 10 | 12 | 14 | 16 | 18 | 20 |

Find the counting pattern. Write the missing numbers.

10	20	30	40	50	60	70	80	90	100
4	8	12	16	20	24	28	32	36	40
37	39	41	43	45	47	49	51	53	55
15	20	25	30	35	40	45	50	55	60
21	22	23	24	25	26	27	28	29	30
7	14	21	28	35	42	49	56	63	70
23	21	19	17	15	13	11	9	7	5
11	22	33	44	55	66	77	88	99	110
100	200	300	400	500	600	700	800	900	1,000
8	16	24	32	40	48	56	64	72	80
12	11	10	9	8	7	6	5	4	3
74	70	66	62	58	54	50	46	42	6

It may be necessary to point out that some of the patterns show an increase and some a decrease. Children should see what operation turns a number into the next number in a pattern, and then repeat the operation to continue the pattern.

53

Adding

Write the answer in the box.

Peter Parker has 46 comics. Venom has 35 comics. How many comics do they have altogether? **81**

Write the answer in the box.

Peter Parker has 42¢ and finds another 22¢. How much does he have in all? **64¢**

What is the total when 47 is added to 48? **95**

Hulk has 33¢ and Iron Man has 29¢. How much do they have altogether? **62¢**

One of Iron Man's safes contains 12 bars of gold. A second safe contains 18 bars of gold. How many bars are there altogether? **30**

Nick Fury captures 34 criminals and Captain Marvel captures 34 criminals. How many criminals did they catch together? **68**

Thor spends 99¢ on a comic and then 38¢ on candy. How much does he spend altogether? **137¢**

Tony Stark finds 12¢ in one pocket and 75¢ in his other pocket. How much does he have altogether? **87¢**

Black Widow has 2 Widow Gauntlets in her bag and 58 at home. How many Gauntlets does she have altogether? **70**

A line is 23 inches long. Peter Parker adds another 25 inches to the line. How long is the line now? **48 in.**

A solar system contains 40 icy planets and 20 gassy planets. How many planets are in the system altogether? **60**

What is the total when 8 is added to 38? **46**

Three spies add their money together. They have $22, $12, and $28. How much do the spies have altogether? **$62**

There are 34 S.H.I.E.L.D agents in one helicopter and 36 agents in another. How many agents are there in total? **70**

A pencil 10 cm long is put end to end with another pencil 12 cm long. What is the total length of the two pencils? **22 cm**

What is the total when 66 is added to 16? **82**

Ideally, children should work out these problems in their head, but you should allow them to write the addition problems out in vertical form if they find it easier.

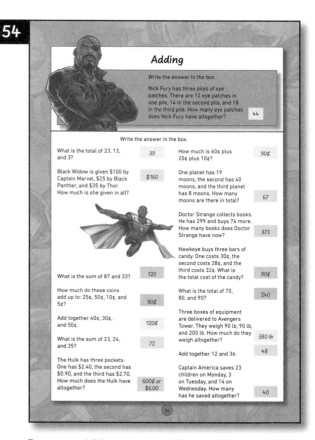

54

Adding

Write the answer in the box.

Nick Fury has three piles of eye patches. There are 12 eye patches in one pile, 14 in the second pile, and 18 in the third pile. How many eye patches does Nick Fury have altogether? **44**

Write the answer in the box.

What is the total of 23, 13, and 3? **39**

How much is 60¢ plus 20¢ plus 10¢? **90¢**

Black Widow is given $100 by Captain Marvel, $25 by Black Panther, and $35 by Thor. How much is she given in all? **$160**

One planet has 19 moons, the second has 40 moons, and the third planet has 8 moons. How many moons are there in total? **67**

Doctor Strange collects books. He has 299 and buys 74 more. How many books does Doctor Strange have now? **373**

Hawkeye buys three bars of candy. One costs 30¢, the second costs 28¢, and the third costs 32¢. What is the total cost of the candy? **90¢**

What is the sum of 87 and 33? **120**

How much do these coins add up to: 25¢, 50¢, 10¢, and 5¢? **90¢**

What is the total of 70, 80, and 90? **240**

Add together 40¢, 30¢, and 50¢. **120¢**

What is the sum of 23, 24, and 25? **72**

Three boxes of equipment are delivered to Avengers Tower. They weigh 90 lb, 90 lb, and 200 lb. How much do they weigh altogether? **380 lb**

Add together 12 and 36. **48**

The Hulk has three pockets. One has $2.40, the second has $0.90, and the third has $2.70. How much does the Hulk have altogether? **600¢ or $6.00**

Captain America saves 23 children on Monday, 3 on Tuesday, and 14 on Wednesday. How many has he saved altogether? **40**

Encourage children to work out these problems mentally. Some of the questions with three addends include two that add up to a multiple of ten. This makes the mental math easier. Children should try to spot these addends.

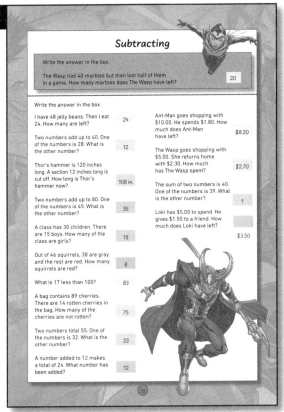

Subtracting

Write the answer in the box.

The Wasp had 40 marbles but then lost half of them in a game. How many marbles does The Wasp have left?
`20`

Write the answer in the box.

I have 48 jelly beans. Then I eat 24. How many are left?
`24`

Two numbers add up to 40. One of the numbers is 28. What is the other number?
`12`

Thor's hammer is 120 inches long. A section 12 inches long is cut off. How long is Thor's hammer now?
`108 in.`

Two numbers add up to 80. One of the numbers is 45. What is the other number?
`35`

A class has 30 children. There are 15 boys. How many of the class are girls?
`15`

Out of 46 squirrels, 38 are gray and the rest are red. How many squirrels are red?
`8`

What is 17 less than 100?
`83`

A bag contains 89 cherries. There are 14 rotten cherries in the bag. How many of the cherries are not rotten?
`75`

Two numbers total 55. One of the numbers is 32. What is the other number?
`23`

A number added to 12 makes a total of 24. What number has been added?
`12`

Ant-Man goes shopping with $10.00. He spends $1.80. How much does Ant-Man have left?
`$8.20`

The Wasp goes shopping with $5.00. She returns home with $2.30. How much has The Wasp spent?
`$2.70`

The sum of two numbers is 40. One of the numbers is 39. What is the other number?
`1`

Loki has $5.00 to spend. He gives $1.50 to a friend. How much does Loki have left?
`$3.50`

Ideally, children should work out these subtraction problems mentally, but you should allow them to write the problems in a vertical form if they find it easier.

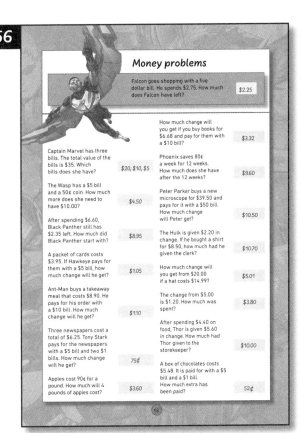

Money problems

Falcon goes shopping with a five dollar bill. He spends $2.75. How much does Falcon have left?
`$2.25`

Captain Marvel has three bills. The total value of the bills is $35. Which bills does she have?
`$20, $10, $5`

The Wasp has a $5 bill and a 50¢ coin. How much more does she need to have $10.00?
`$4.50`

After spending $6.60, Black Panther still has $2.35 left. How much did Black Panther start with?
`$8.95`

A packet of cards costs $3.95. If Hawkeye pays for them with a $5 bill, how much change will he get?
`$1.05`

Ant-Man buys a takeaway meal that costs $8.90. He pays for his order with a $10 bill. How much change will he get?
`$1.10`

Three newspapers cost a total of $6.25. Tony Stark pays for the newspapers with a $5 bill and two $1 bills. How much change will he get?
`75¢`

Apples cost 90¢ for a pound. How much will 4 pounds of apples cost?
`$3.60`

How much change will you get if you buy books for $6.68 and pay for them with a $10 bill?
`$3.32`

Phoenix saves 80¢ a week for 12 weeks. How much does she have after the 12 weeks?
`$9.60`

Peter Parker buys a new microscope for $39.50 and pays for it with a $50 bill. How much change will Peter get?
`$10.50`

The Hulk is given $2.20 in change. If he bought a shirt for $8.50, how much had he given the clerk?
`$10.70`

How much change will you get from $20.00 if a hat costs $14.99?
`$5.01`

The change from $5.00 is $1.20. How much was spent?
`$3.80`

After spending $4.40 on food, Thor is given $5.60 in change. How much had Thor given to the storekeeper?
`$10.00`

A box of chocolates costs $5.48. It is paid for with a $5 bill and a $1 bill. How much extra has been paid?
`52¢`

These questions involve money in realistic situations. Children must choose between addition and subtraction to solve each problem.

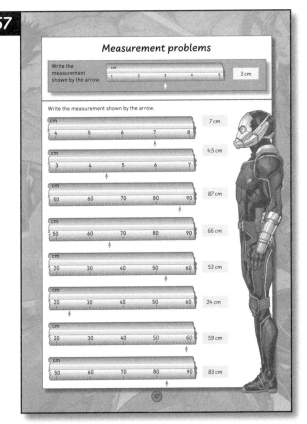

Measurement problems

Write the measurement shown by the arrow.
`3 cm`

Write the measurement shown by the arrow.

`7 cm`

`4.5 cm`

`87 cm`

`66 cm`

`53 cm`

`24 cm`

`59 cm`

`83 cm`

Children should be able to read off scales of this type relatively easily. Make sure that children include the units in their answers.

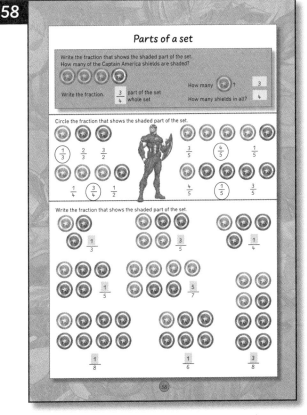

Parts of a set

Write the fraction that shows the shaded part of the set. How many of the Captain America shields are shaded?

Write the fraction. $\frac{3}{4}$ part of the set whole set

How many ? `3`
How many shields in all? `4`

Circle the fraction that shows the shaded part of the set.

$\frac{1}{3}$ $\frac{2}{3}$ $\frac{3}{2}$

$\frac{3}{5}$ $\frac{4}{5}$ $\frac{1}{5}$

$\frac{1}{4}$ $\frac{3}{4}$ $\frac{1}{2}$

$\frac{4}{5}$ $\frac{1}{5}$ $\frac{3}{5}$

Write the fraction that shows the shaded part of the set.

$\frac{1}{3}$

$\frac{3}{5}$

$\frac{1}{4}$

$\frac{1}{5}$

$\frac{5}{7}$

$\frac{1}{8}$

$\frac{1}{6}$

$\frac{3}{8}$

If children have difficulty, point out that the denominator—bottom number of the fraction—is the total number of parts. The numerator—or top part of the fraction—is the number of shaded parts.

Bar graphs and pictographs

Look at the bar graph and answer the question.

HOW MANY CARDS?

Who has three cards? | Hulk

Look at the bar graph and answer the questions.

CRIMINALS CAUGHT

How many criminals did Iron Man catch? | 6
Who caught eight criminals? | Spidey
Who caught fewer criminals than Thor? | Hulk
Who caught the most criminals? | Ant-Man
How many criminals were caught in total? | 30

Look at the pictograph and answer the questions.

CHILDREN'S FAVORITE SUPER HEROES

each badge stands for 2 children

| Iron Man | Hulk | Black Widow | Captain America |

How many children like Captain America the most? | 2
Which Super Hero is the favorite of 5 children? | Black Widow
How many more children like Iron Man than the Hulk? | 2
Who is the most popular Super Hero? | Iron Man

Children should notice that the units on the bar graph scale are in twos rather than ones, as are the icons on the pictograph. To answer some of the questions, children will have to add and compare data.

Symmetry

Some of these shapes have lines of symmetry in unusual positions. Let children use mirrors on the shapes if they are unsure of their answers. Or, they can trace the drawing onto white paper, then fold the paper to see if both sides of the figure match.

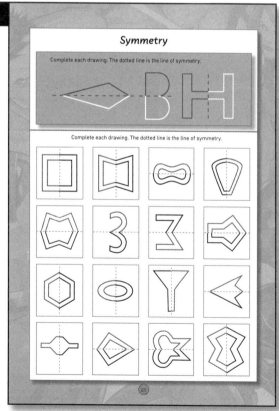

Symmetry

Complete each drawing. The dotted line is the line of symmetry.

Let children use mirrors if they are unsure about any of their drawings. Or, children can trace the drawing onto white paper, then fold the paper to see if both sides of the figure match and to find the line of symmetry.

Doubles

Write the missing numbers.

Double it
7 → 14
6 → 12
2 → 4

Double it
3 → 6
5 → 10
9 → 18

Double it
5 → 10
0 → 0
1 → 2

Double it
4 → 8
11 → 22
8 → 16

What has been doubled? Write the missing number.

Double 5 is 10   Double 2 4

Double 3 is 6   Double 11 is 22   Double 5 is 10
Double 4 is 8   Double 9 is 18   Double 7 is 14
Double 0 is 0   Double 1 is 2

Explain that doubling is the same as adding two sets of the same number. If children cannot yet double in their head, use counters to make two sets of the number, and add them.

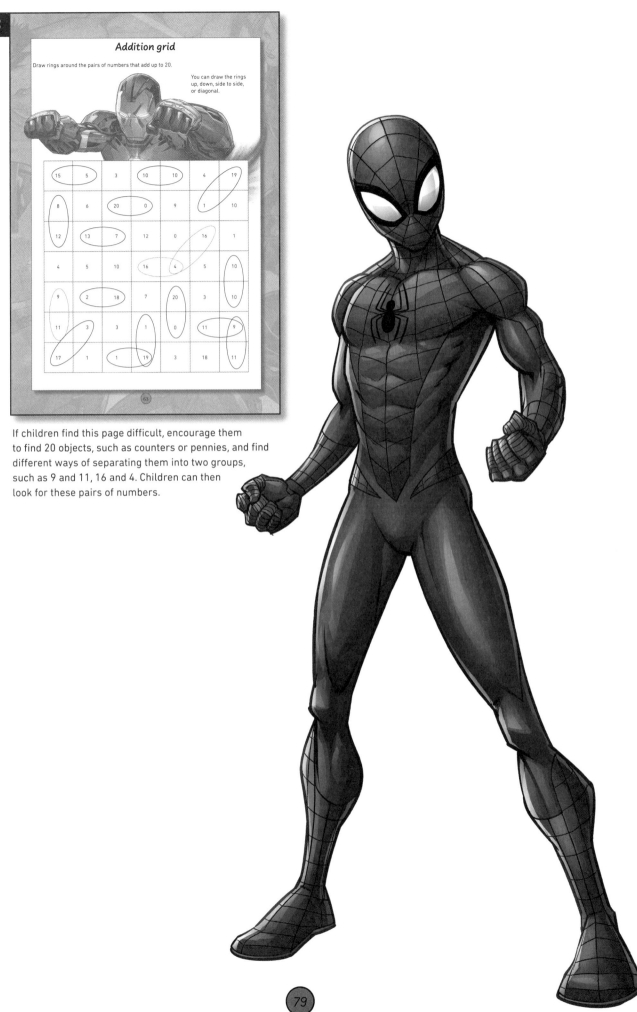

Addition grid

Draw rings around the pairs of numbers that add up to 20.

You can draw the rings up, down, side to side, or diagonal.

15	5	3	10	10	4	19
8	6	20	0	9	1	10
12	13	7	12	0	16	1
4	5	10	16	4	5	10
9	2	18	7	20	3	10
11	3	3	1	0	11	9
17	1	1	19	3	18	11

If children find this page difficult, encourage them to find 20 objects, such as counters or pennies, and find different ways of separating them into two groups, such as 9 and 11, 16 and 4. Children can then look for these pairs of numbers.

Senior Editor Emma Grange
Editoral Assistant Vicky Armstrong
Project Art Editor Chris Gould
Designer Thelma-Jane Robb
Senior Production Controller Louise Minihane
Senior Production Editor Jennifer Murray
Managing Editor Sarah Harland
Managing Art Editor Vicky Short
Publisher Julie Ferris
Art Director Lisa Lanzarini
Publishing Director Mark Searle

First American Edition, 2020
Published in the United States
by DK Publishing
1450 Broadway, Suite 801, New York, NY 10018

20 21 22 23 24 10 9 8 7 6 5 4 3 2 1
001-323463-Oct/2020

Page design copyright © 2020
Dorling Kindersley Limited
DK, a division of Penguin Random House LLC

Contains content previously published in *Marvel Heroes Math Made Easy 2nd Grade* (2007)

A catalog record for this book is available from the Library of Congress.

ISBN: 978-0-7440-3703-6

DK books are available at special discounts when purchased in bulk
for sales promotions, premiums, fundraising, or educational use. For details,
contact: DK Publishing Special Markets, 1450 Broadway, Suite 801,
New York, NY 10018
SpecialSales@dk.com

Printed and bound in China

For the curious

www.dk.com